Albee: Who's Afraid of Virginia Woolf?

This is the first detailed study of one of the most important plays in contemporary theatre, *Who's Afraid of Virginia Woolf?*, by Edward Albee. In this fascinating look at the modern stage, Stephen Bottoms draws on archival material and original sources including an exclusive interview with Edward Albee. The Introduction considers the text of the play itself; part one provides a survey of the major productions from 1962 to 1999, with special attention paid to the premiere and the 1966 film version. Part two examines shifting critical responses to the play, demonstrating how changing times and attitudes have altered audience perception of performances. The third and final part offers a detailed examination of five different performances, comparing and contrasting directorial, design and acting approaches to demonstrate how our understanding of the play alters considerably according to its interpretation on stage.

ALBEE

Who's Afraid of Virginia Woolf?

WITHDRAWN

PLAYS IN PRODUCTION

Series editor: Michael Robinson

PUBLISHED VOLUMES

ALBEE

Who's Afraid of Virginia Woolf?

*

STEPHEN J. BOTTOMS
University of Glasgow

CAMBRIDGE
UNIVERSITY PRESS

PUBLISHED BY THE PRESS SYNDICATE OF THE UNIVERSITY OF CAMBRIDGE
The Pitt Building, Trumpington Street, Cambridge, United Kingdom

CAMBRIDGE UNIVERSITY PRESS
The Edinburgh Building, Cambridge CB2 2RU, UK   www.cup.cam.ac.uk
40 West 20th Street, New York, NY 10011–4211, USA   www.cup.org
10 Stamford Road, Oakleigh, Melbourne 3166, Australia
Ruiz de Alarcón 13, 28014 Madrid, Spain

First published 2000

Printed in the United Kingdom at the University Press, Cambridge

Typeface Adobe Garamond 10.75/14   *System* QuarkXPress™   [SE]

A catalogue record for this book is available from the British Library

Library of Congress Cataloguing in Publication data

Bottoms, Stephen J. (Stephen James), 1968–
Albee : Who's afraid of Virginia Woolf? / Stephen J. Bottoms.
p.   cm. – (Plays in production)
Includes bibliographical references and index.
ISBN 0 521 63209 9 – ISBN 0 521 63560 8 (pbk.)
1. Albee, Edward, 1928 – Who's afraid of Virginia Woolf?   2. Albee, Edward, 1928 –
Film and video adaptations.   3. Albee, Edward, 1928 – Dramatic production.   4.
Albee, Edward, 1928 – Stage history.   5. Married people in literature.   I. Title.
II. Series.

PS3551.L25 W434 2000   812'.54–dc21   99-056106

ISBN 0 521 63209 9 hardback
ISBN 0 521 63560 8 paperback

for Doric and the dancing lady

CONTENTS

ILLUSTRATIONS

Photographs 1, 2, 3, 4, 6, 7, and 9 are by Friedman / Abeles and reproduced courtesy of the Billy Rose Theatre Collection, The New York Public Library for the Performing Arts, and the Astor, Lenox, and Tilden Foundations

GENERAL PREFACE

Volumes in the series Plays in Production take major dramatic texts and examine their transposition, firstly on to the stage and, secondly, where appropriate, into other media. Each book includes concise but informed studies of individual dramatic texts, focusing on the original theatrical and historical context of a play in relation to its initial performance and reception followed by subsequent major interpretations on stage, both under the impact of changing social, political and cultural values, and in response to developments in the theatre generally.

Many of the plays will also have been transposed into other media – film, opera, television, ballet – which may well be the form in which they are first encountered by a contemporary audience. Thus, a substantial study of the play-text and the issues it raises for theatrical realisation is supplemented by an assessment of such adaptations as well as the production history, where the emphasis is on the development of a performance tradition for each work, including staging and acting styles, rather than simply the archaeological reconstruction of past performances.

Plays included in the series are all likely to receive regular performance and individual volumes will be of interest to the informed reader as well as to students of theatre history and literature. Each book also contains an annotated production chronology as well as numerous photographs from key performances.

Michael Robinson
University of East Anglia

ACKNOWLEDGEMENTS

I would like to express my enormous gratitude to all of these interviewees for their invaluable contributions. My further thanks go to Mr Albee for his generosity in allowing me to consult the closed archive of his unpublished and draft manuscripts, held by the Billy Rose Theatre Collection, Lincoln Center Library for the Performing Arts, New York City. The archivists of the Billy Rose Collection are also due a big thankyou, as are those at the National Sound Archive of the British Library, which granted me permission to consult three sound recordings of performances of *Virginia Woolf* (1963 CBS original cast recording; 1974 BBC radio version; 1981 National Theatre production), and at the Research Collection of the London Theatre Museum, where I was able to view for the videotape recording of the 1996 Almeida production.

I would also like to acknowledge my debt to the research conducted by Andrew B. Harris and Susan Spector, whose previously published writings on the 1962 premiere proved particularly valuable as source material. The same goes for Leonard J. Leff's work on the 1966 movie version. My personal thanks also to the following people for their advice and assistance during my own writing process: Mark Batty, David Crespy, Paula Rabbitt, Christopher Robinson, Brian Woolland, and – at Cambridge University Press – Victoria Cooper and Michael Robinson. Finally, I should acknowledge the work of two successive groups of final year Theatre Studies students at the University of Glasgow, who foolishly decided to sit a 'specialist research option' on '*Who's Afraid of Virginia Woolf?* in production', and became unwitting collaborators in developing some of the thoughts set out in the following chapters. My appreciation and apologies go to all of you.

NOTE ON THE TEXT

I have used the author–date system in annotating this volume, giving full publication details for works in the list of references. Please note, however, that to avoid cluttering the text with unnecessary citations, no parenthesised details are given in cases where the reference is already clear from comments in the main text. For example, newspaper reviews are referred to simply by citing the critic's name in the main text, if the year of publication is the same as the year of the production referred to, and if the review's single page reference is already in the bibliography. The exception to this rule is where reviews are referenced with the abbreviation *LTR*, for *London Theatre Record* – the cuttings journal which I have consulted for reviews of the 1981, 1987 and 1996 London productions. Here page references apply to the *Record*, since it does not list original page details.

All citations from the playtext itself are noted simply with parenthetical page numbers, which refer to the standard Penguin edition (Harmondsworth 1965; endlessly reprinted). Please note also that where quotations from theatre practitioners are not otherwise attributed, they are drawn from the following personal interviews, which were conducted during my research for this book:

Edward Albee	Edinburgh, 19 September 1997
Howard Davies	London, 1 February 1998
Clare Holman	London, 1 February 1998
Elizabeth McCann	New York, 2 February 1997
Nancy Meckler	London, 16 March 1998
Doric Wilson	New York, 15 February 1997

INTRODUCTION
THE PLAY AS PERFORMANCE

It's odd isn't it that so many contemporary playwrights are best known for one play, usually an early one and, while often a very good one, not necessarily their finest work . . . I find *Who's Afraid of Virginia Woolf?* hung about my neck like a shining medal of some sort – really nice but a trifle onerous. Living playwrights bridle a little at this sort of short-hand, for we all insist – hope? – that we haven't written our best works yet, and we all harbour deep, almost religious faith in our most dismissed and despised efforts . . . Please don't misunderstand me: I'm very happy to have written *Who's Afraid of Virginia Woolf?* I think it's a fine play . . . and if there is a history years from now, and if I am a footnote in it, I daresay *Who's Afraid of Virginia Woolf?* will be the play identified with my name (or my name with it), and I, in my shallow grave, will not cavil much. (*Albee 1996*)

These words of Edward Albee, taken from the programme note he contributed for the 1996 London production of *Who's Afraid of Virginia Woolf?*, suggest more than a little ambivalence on the author's part toward being asked to comment on yet another revival. While it was clearly gratifying to be back 'in vogue' following the international success of *Three Tall Women* (his 1994 Pulitzer Prize-winner), the resulting succession of revivals of his best-known plays, on both sides of the Atlantic, also prompted a degree of wryly resigned reflection on the continuing neglect of some of his lesser-known 'children'. This attitude was also apparent when I interviewed Albee in Edinburgh in September 1997, while he was attending previews for a revival of *A Delicate Balance*. He graciously and carefully answered all my questions about *Virginia Woolf*, but it would plainly

1

have been more refreshing for him to be asked to talk about, say, *The Man Who Had Three Arms*, the Broadway premiere of which closed after a mere sixteen performances in 1983, and which he cites as his most underrated play.

Why then this book? Does a study of *Who's Afraid of Virginia Woolf?* in production add anything fresh to the amassed critical material already published on Albee's most famous play? It is not, after all, a piece which invites particularly radical variations in the way it is presented in production. There are only so many ways one can stage a four-character play set in a living-room without departing from the author's guidelines for production, and, since the author is still alive and well and rigorously vigilant about policing major productions to see that his intentions are observed, there is little scope for the kind of auteurist directorial re-visioning now so often applied to classic texts, both ancient and modern. Nevertheless, while the variations among productions of *Virginia Woolf* may be subtler than those among productions of many other plays, it is a text which provides extraordinarily rich material for the line-by-line exploration of motivation, inflection, reaction. This may not be a play for auteurs, but it is, supremely, one for actors, and it is in the subtleties of their performances that the sometimes quite marked variations between productions make themselves most apparent. A detailed examination of the varying interpretations of this play onstage can reveal a great deal about both the text and the actors who have played it – among whom are numbered some of the greatest performers of modern times, from Uta Hagen to Diana Rigg, Richard Burton to Paul Eddington, Colleen Dewhurst to Billie Whitelaw.

Beyond this, however, I believe that a critical production history of *Who's Afraid of Virginia Woolf?* is important precisely *because* it is such a well-known and discussed play. For this approach requires that one look not only at the staging of the text itself, but also into the way productions have been received, and why. These issues have been largely overlooked in the various critical debates over the play, but such an examination is vital in beginning to appreciate why it has achieved the status of 'modern classic' which it now enjoys (or, perhaps, is burdened with). The play did not spring from its author's head full-formed as a cultural landmark; it became one in the light of interpretive responses not only from actors but from *audiences.* Indeed, without denigrating Albee's achievement as a writer by one iota, I would suggest that his play's appearance in 1962, at a particular, pivotal moment in America's cultural and theatrical history, is of at least at much significance to the status it now holds as what he actually put on the page. It was a series of highly publicised and highly controversial productions which secured the play's public reputation – most notably the original Broadway production with Uta Hagen and the 1966 movie version with Elizabeth Taylor and Richard Burton (then at the height of their tabloid-selling fame). It was inevitable that these productions – with their numerous 'x factors' of performances, reputations, hype, and media reaction – were extremely influential in shaping subsequent perceptions of the play itself. A production history of *Who's Afraid of Virginia Woolf?* is thus a history not only of a play-text, but of a cultural artefact written over by many more hands than Albee's alone.

With these points in mind, I have divided this book into three, interrelated chapters. The first is a nuts-and-bolts history of how the play came to be staged, first on Broadway and then around the world. I look also at how it came to be filmed, and the controversies that resulted from the filming, before looking, finally, at details of some of the major revivals of the play. (Together these stories feature as much intrigue, strategising and backstabbing as an evening at Martha and George's.) Chapter two is a kind of critical biography of the play, an examination of the reactions to its various incarnations which endeavours to account for some of the cultural-historical factors which have played such a significant role in shaping the way the play is perceived. The third chapter turns the spotlight on the choices which directors, designers and especially actors have made in crafting specific performances of *Virginia Woolf,* by comparing and contrasting several key productions dating between 1962 and 1996. As this last section makes particularly clear, it has been necessary to delimit the scope of the book's concerns somewhat, since a study like this could not possibly do justice to all the major productions of *Virginia Woolf* worldwide over thirty-five years. I have therefore focused primarily on key productions in the United States and the United Kingdom, while also making reference to foreign-language productions of particular relevance to my general arguments. As a British scholar of American theatre, this approach reflects my own cultural myopia, but it has also allowed for an in-depth examination of the play's impact in its original English in these two closely related cultures.

Before continuing, I want briefly to map out a few of the other prejudices which have informed the writing of this book. The notion that one could provide a 'neutral' or 'impartial' history of a play in production is deeply suspect, and since I have made no pretence at such omniscience it is important to acknowledge the assumptions I have worked from. What follows is informed, in particular, by the conviction that *Who's Afraid of Virginia Woolf?* is a play which demands to be seen in performance to be fully appreciated. This might not seem very controversial, but it does contradict somewhat Albee's own repeated assertion that 'with a good play – anybody's good play – seeing it on stage is merely a proof of what exists on the page and not an improvement on it, not a completion of it, merely a proof of it' (Kolin 1988: 137). While acknowledging that there are a number of legitimate ways to perform a play like *Virginia Woolf*, which may suggest different readings – 'there's more than one way to skin a cat' – Albee insists that it can be as well appreciated on the page. I believe that this is true of many of his later plays, and indeed that their literary subtlety can easily be lost in performance if not handled by experts. Yet *Virginia Woolf* is unceasingly popular with audiences precisely because it is the most theatrically dynamic of all Albee's plays; not in the sense of offering spectacle or provocative staging conceits (several of his other works are much more suggestive in this regard), but in the sense of characters using words as weapons in a running battle for control of the stage situation. This play is compulsive viewing in the truest sense, setting up what one early reviewer called a 'shamefully funny, hideously watchable' series of games and confrontations (Hope-Wallace 1964). Strangely, my clearest memory of my own first experience of seeing *Virginia Woolf* in production, in a low-budget student venture, is of the play's two intervals (not something you can experience on the page), simply because they felt like momentary respites in which to gasp for air before being plunged back into the thrilling, scalding confusion of the performance. To revert to Albee's own choice of cliché, reading about a cat being skinned is not at all the same thing as watching it happen in front of you.

By way of expanding on these observations, I would argue that *Who's Afraid of Virginia Woolf?* not only demands to be performed, but is a play which is, fundamentally, *all about* performance and per- formativity. This notion of the 'performative' has been taken up, in recent years, as a key theoretical issue in many fields besides that of theatre studies, relating as it does to the operations of language which affect us all on a day-to-day basis. The touchstone for all such investi- gations is a seminal collection of lectures by the British philosopher J. L. Austin, published under the playfully simplistic title *How to Do Things with Words* in 1962. (It seems almost too perfect a coincidence that *Who's Afraid of Virginia Woolf?* premiered in the same year.) Austin's argument hinges on the suggestion that, in addition to using language to make 'constative' statements to convey information about our world to our listeners, we also use language performatively, to enact actual changes in that world. 'I dare you.' 'I beg you.' 'I do.' Crucially, though, this distinction between the constative and perfor- mative has since been queried by other writers, most notably Jacques Derrida, who deconstructs Austin's binary opposition by pointing out (and here I am necessarily over-simplifying) that even the most appar- ently innocuous constative statement *performs* some active purpose by demonstrating knowledge on the speaker's part, and conveying that information in a manner angled to create a desired response in the listener. Derrida thus stresses, in line with many of his other writings, that language is an unstable, deceptive tool which can never simply be taken at face value; that the traditional question of whether an utterance is 'true' or 'false' is over-simplistic, and often of far less value than analysing what kind of *impact* it has. The upshot of Austin's work, Derrida suggests, is to 'free the analysis of the performative from the value of truth, from the opposition true/false', and to refocus attention on 'the value of force' (Derrida 1982: 322).

Who's Afraid of Virginia Woolf?, I would argue, enacts a similar shift of emphasis in the context of the drama. By blurring the supposed line between reality and invention via the tricksiness, malice and increasing intoxication of his characters, Albee plays havoc with the conventional assumption that realistic dramaturgy operates to reveal the 'truth' of the situation depicted and of the characters' motivations. Instead, he refocuses attention on the impact of performative interaction, as the climax of the play, in particular, makes startlingly explicit. Martha is reduced to despair by George's announcement of the death of their imaginary son ('I have killed him'), not because she actually believes in this as a physical murder (she is not insane), but because she knows that George's performative decree has had the effect of taking them across a line which cannot be re-crossed. Indeed, like an actor coming out of character, she even tries desperately to 'block' this latest twist in their improvisation: 'YOU . . . CAN'T . . . DO . . . THAT!' (135).

Unquestionably, *Virginia Woolf* owes a great deal to the example of European writers such as Pirandello, Genet and, of course, Beckett, with their varying takes on the notion that a drama stripped of a plot might be a peculiarly apt metaphor for life – leaving the characters to make themselves up, act themselves out, as they go. Albee's key innovation here, however, was to apply the principle of theatrical game-playing to a situation which appears on the surface to be entirely naturalistic, rather than writing in a more overtly avant-garde or experimental manner. Harold Pinter had already attempted something similar, but his characters remained oblique, unsettling, set at a distance from the spectator. By contrast, a major source of *Virginia Woolf*'s extraordinary impact on audiences is the fact that its initial premise and characters seem immediately recognisable and accessible, but that it then breaks the habituated 'rules' of naturalism by preventing the spectator from coming to any reliable understanding of the past events shaping George and Martha's present turmoil. Did George really kill both his parents, for example, as is implied by the stories he tells Nick and Honey? Or is this simply another level of deception, another game? Critics have debated these points at length, but ultimately what seems clear is that discovering the truth or falsity of such 'revelations' is beside the point: in a contingent world where there are no final answers, it is the impact that George's *performance* has on his listeners that is of greater significance – the very real power of his words to shock, to intimidate, to conjure an emotional response.

George, of all the play's characters, is the most shrewdly aware of 'how to do things with words'. Throughout the evening, he contravenes the usually unquestioned conventions of linguistic intercourse for the sake of both comedy and control. In his first one-on-one encounter with Nick, for example, he deliberately interprets an innocuous figure of speech over-literally, so as to make his 'guest' still more uncomfortable than he is already:

> GEORGE: What made you decide to be a teacher?
> NICK: Oh . . . well . . . the same things that . . . uh . . . motivated you, I imagine.
> GEORGE: What were they?
> NICK [*formal*]: Pardon?
> GEORGE: I said, what were they? What were the things that motivated me?
> NICK [*laughing uneasily*]: Well . . . I'm sure I don't know. (*25*)

Martha, by contrast, tends to operate more by declaration than by subversion, but her words are no less effective, often building into tirades of near-bludgeoning force. A prime example would be the speech with which she combats George's Latin rite of 'exorcism' in the last act, with its insistently rhythmic use of repetition:

> I have tried, oh God I have tried; the one thing . . . the one thing I have tried to carry pure and unscathed through the sewer of this marriage; through the sick nights, and the pathetic, stupid days, through the derision and the laughter . . . *God*, the laughter, through one failure after another, one failure compounding another failure, each attempt more sickening, more numbing than the one before; the one thing, the one *person* I have tried to protect, to raise above the mire of this vile, crushing marriage; the one light in all this hopeless . . . *dark*ness . . . our SON. (*132–3*)

Clearly Martha does not actually need all these words to make her point, since in literal terms what she is saying is actually very simple. Yet the manner in which she says it is incantatory: the speech deals not in truth or falsity (except insofar as she is perhaps trying to convince herself as much as her listeners of the veracity of her sentiment), but in *momentum*, building toward an attempt at the kind of finality which brooks no contradiction. George, however, simultaneously attempts to undermine her words by quietly reciting the Latin of the requiem Mass. Hands to her ears, Honey responds by screaming for both Martha and George to stop: the combined *effect* of their words is, quite simply, maddening.

Timothy Gould's summation of J. L. Austin's work could also stand as a useful summary of Albee's play: 'Delivering us from the old fetishism of the true and false would, by the same act, deliver us over to what the fetish was perhaps designed to conceal: a more homely, less manageable, and hence more uncanny region – a region in which our utterances find (or fail to find) their various relations to the world and its other inhabitants' (Parker and Sedgwick 1995: 24). The theatrical culture in which *Who's Afraid of Virginia Woolf?* first appeared was not, however, in any way prepared for transport to such territory, and – since first impressions are all too often recycled later as conventional wisdom – the objections raised at that time have continued to haunt Albee ever since. The production history of *Virginia Woolf* has been partially characterised by persistent complaints, from newspaper reviewers in particular, that this is a severely flawed piece of work.

The major objections to the play have been twofold: first, that at three to three-and-a-half hours running time on stage it is unnecessarily long and repetitive, that the same 'point' could have been made in a much shorter space of time (the success of the much shorter film version has been taken by some as proof of this, despite the fundamental differences in the media involved); second, that the scenario of George and Martha's imaginary child is a crude piece of symbolism tacked on to the end of the play to hammer home the 'point'. Both complaints are grounded in the unquestioned assumption that the play (in the tradition of liberal realism) exists to *make* a point, to propagate a message, to *utter a constative*, and that the form via which this content is communicated to the audience is therefore of secondary and ultimately disposable importance. 'By reducing the work of art to its content and then interpreting *that*, one tames the work of art', Susan Sontag wrote in 1964: 'Real art has the capacity to make us nervous' (Sontag 1964: 99). The very length of *Virginia Woolf*, as other observers have pointed out, is in fact central to its performative impact on an audience: it is, as Max Lerner once put it, Albee's use of the 'exactly irrelevant word . . . the seemingly aimless zigzagging of the conversation and the action, of the imaginative soarings of fancy and fantasy . . . that leave[s] you bemused, bedazzled, and bedeviled' (Lerner 1962).

Of course *Who's Afraid of Virginia Woolf?* does deal with thematic content, functioning – in particular – as a kind of political comment on the corruption of American values, and as a philosophical reflection on the nature of illusion. These ideas are built into the fabric of the play in such a way as to prevent them being reducible to a simple statement or message. Yet the critical tendency has been to reduce them anyway. References to Albee's 'sophomoric philosophising' have been commonplace in reviews of

Virginia Woolf from the outset, and certain pat summaries of the play's concerns make repeated appearances in even some of the more appreciative critical appraisals. For example, Albee's decision to name his protagonists after America's first (childless) presidential family has often been taken as being central to the play's claims to profundity – and this despite the author's admission that the choice was little more than a playful provocation (there was, he says, 'some notion in my mind' when writing the play that 'there might be an allegory to be drawn' from the characters' names, but 'it's not terribly important' [McCarthy 1987: 66]). The standard interpretive gloss, as summarised by Walter Kerr, is that George and Martha's 'illusory offspring . . . first fought over and then permitted to die, is indeed the vaunted American dream, given spurious birth by the legend of the Washingtons, hotly debated thereafter, now dead'. And yet, Kerr notes scathingly in his review of the 1976 Broadway revival,

> as we watch the sparks fly and feel the heat from the evening's anvil, we realize that this is so much nonsense. Symbolically, the exegesis doesn't work. It *never* occurs to us, as we take relish in the very personal infighting, that we are attending the creation and demise of anything so abstract, so remote, so specifically political, so unfleshed. If it did occur to us, we shouldn't see the relevance. . . [George and Martha's] bitter story is both larger and deeper than facile, two-dimensional political cartooning. (*Kerr 1976*)

Kerr's comments are insightful, but they also serve to *de*politicise the play, to paint it simply as a domestic 'situation', a reading which seems to me as problematic as the simplistic readings he is mocking. The political dimension of the play is at once much more integral to the events as a whole than is the scheme Kerr outlines, and far less easily summarised. For Howard Davies, director of the 1996 London revival, Albee is 'fundamentally . . . a political writer', because his concerns with history and power relations are written into the very grain of his characters' performative confrontations:

I've directed a lot of American plays, and I'm fascinated by the way that the politics of American dramaturgy is limited either to a bar – *Time of Your Life, Iceman Cometh* – or to the family . . . and its problems in terms of how you hang together sexually, morally, politically . . . That's the metaphor, the political metaphor, and *Who's Afraid of Virginia Woolf?* is simply perfect, because it's a quartet . . . We all know situations where in any relationship or any marriage you find yourself in a position where people start playing out their anger with their partner through their guests, at the other person's expense. It's deeply uncomfortable. And parents do it with their children, they use them as pawns to be moved about in their psychological or emotional battleground to achieve maximum points . . . And the fundamental line that's contained in the play is that this child doesn't exist. These people are constructed in a war zone and then are exposed as having no future.

Davies thus ties the play's exposure of the emptiness underlying George and Martha's brutal machinations to a broader political reading, while also pointing back towards that 'uncanny region' lying beyond trivialising statements or messages, which the play moves its audience towards with such unsettling momentum.

It might be objected, of course, that Albee has himself periodically participated in the trivialisation of the play. (Indeed, Walter Kerr's cited comments were explicitly a response to remarks attributed to the author by the press.) Such objections, however, overlook Albee's career-long insistence that any play which can be summed up in a couple of sentences does not deserve to be any longer than that. Like Samuel Beckett, perhaps Albee's most significant influence, he knows that by focusing insistently on a distilled theatrical situation, the playwright can conjure resonances in the minds of an audience which operate on a level beyond any neat, rational explanations. Yet where Beckett always refused to answer questions about what his plays might mean (insisting that if he had known what Godot represented he would not have needed to write the play), Albee has often adopted a more playful approach. In line with the more overt performativity of his writing, he has merrily invented explanations for those who insist on asking for them – apparently adopting the attitude that such throw-offs will not damage the play itself, since those who want to explore it with open minds will always find much richer rewards in the text. Meanwhile, he has clearly derived a certain amount of entertainment from leading critics up the garden path in their search for one-line meanings. 'I do quite often play games', he admitted when I pushed him on this in interview, all the time smiling wryly as if to tell me that this might be one too:

> BOTTOMS: Games like the George and Martha Washington thing, for instance?
>
> ALBEE: That was fun . . . You get asked to explain things, and you sigh heavily, and eventually – Like they asked me what the title meant, the *title*, and I said, '*Who's afraid of Virginia Woolf?* means who's afraid of the big bad wolf means who's afraid of a life without illusions.' People want over-simplification. I don't know why. But you know, I did name Nick after Nikita Kruschev!
>
> BOTTOMS: Wasn't that just a private joke? Like naming the Western Union delivery guy Crazy Billy?
>
> ALBEE: He was my lover. We both worked for Western Union.
>
> BOTTOMS: Deeply significant to the play.
>
> ALBEE: Very significant, yes.

Albee's throwaway line 'who's afraid of a life without illusion' has repeatedly been taken as the comment which, more than any other, sums up the play's key concerns (rather than a line which riffs playfully on the title). Far more so than the question of political allegory, it is this which is most often seen as the 'message' of the play, and Albee's open acknowledgement that *Virginia Woolf* is, in part, a response to Eugene O'Neill's *The Iceman Cometh* has been interpreted as reinforcing this reading. Since O'Neill's play implies that one needs to hide behind false illusions because the truth (if it is knowable at all) is often too painful to bear, it has often been taken as read that *Virginia Woolf* simply inverts that dichotomy, arguing for the stripping away of false illusions in order that one can confront the truth. Yet this blithely ignores lines within the play such as

George's 'Truth and illusion. Who knows the difference, eh, toots?' (119), and Albee's own repeated insistence that 'I do think people probably need self-deception and lies. The only distinction I would make is that I think people should have them but be aware that they are deceiving themselves' (Kolin 1988: 170).

Another way of phrasing this last remark might be that people need to be aware that they are only ever playing roles they have invented for themselves. As Albee's long-term producer Richard Barr once suggested, 'Edward was the first playwright to say that people invent their own illusion to give themselves a reality. And his characters are *aware* of it . . . A Blanche Dubois doesn't know she's living an illusion. But Edward's characters – certainly those in *Virginia Woolf* and *Tiny Alice* – are aware they're creating the illusion themselves. That's the giant step' (Kolin 1988: 178). For Albee, it seems, acknowledging that one has created illusions for oneself and then continuing to live by them is not an act of bad faith but a necessary form of self-invention, a rejection of the essentialist assumption that there is a 'true self' to be faithful *to*. It is simply to admit that one's take on the world is necessarily performative, that we are composed of the roles we play, the lines we improvise for ourselves. The stripping away of such illusions will not, therefore, necessarily result in the revelation of some hidden layer of underlying truth. It is as likely that another provisional arrangement of fictions will have to be negotiated, as George makes (unnecessarily) explicit in a passage directed at Nick and Honey which Albee chose to delete from the end of the play: 'I would make a suggestion to the two of you: You have within you and between you . . . a possibility. Try to . . . try to, in some way, *establish the basis for a legend*' (quoted Bigsby 1984: 272; my emphasis). Significantly, Albee had used almost exactly the same phrase in reference to another young couple in *The Making of a Saint*, one of his early, unproduced plays of the 1950s.

In short, *Who's Afraid of Virginia Woolf?* does not so much invert O'Neill's dichotomy as dissolve it. In this regard, Richard Barr's mention of *Tiny Alice* makes for an important comparison. Albee's next original play after *Virginia Woolf, Tiny Alice* brilliantly extends his concern with games and role-playing to their logical conclusion: the central character Brother Julian has his sanity shattered by a kind of elaborate, de Sadeian deception, in which the lover in whom he places all his faith turns out to be merely an actress. Any attempt at categorically understanding or explaining experience, Albee implies, is always already a kind of performative fiction, a creative attempt to represent the unrepresentable, which can be dismantled as easily as Brother Julian's take on reality. *Tiny Alice* makes these themes apparent through such striking stage metaphors as the scale replica of Alice's house, which stands within the house we see on stage, which may itself be a replica inside another, giant-sized house we cannot see: which level of reality is the 'real' one? By contrast, *Who's Afraid of Virginia Woolf?* is at once more and less direct, because Albee focuses on the immediate interaction of his characters, on the moment-by-moment playing out of their various games, stories and confrontations, rather than on the explication of thematic paradoxes. To dissolve another dichotomy, the play's 'content' reflects its form, but the form is – in a still more important sense – its content.

If *Virginia Woolf* is indeed 'about' performativity, my demonstration of this argument is on one level simply a theoretical justification for this book's concentration on the play *as* performance. Audiences, after all, find themselves drawn into the play not by philosophical reflections on reality, illusion and role-play but by the cut-and-thrust vitality of the war games being enacted in front of them, the 'meaning' of which is exactly what it appears to be. 'Do you use games as a metaphor for life?' an interviewer asked Albee in 1984. 'I don't think so. I think it's simply that people play games. Subtle and intelligent people play subtle and intelligent games . . . power games, guilt games.' Moreover, he is well aware that playing such games *through* his characters has a direct impact on those sitting beyond the proscenium arch: 'I'm probably aware that it has *a kind of effectiveness* while I'm doing it' (Kolin 1988: 185; my emphasis).

CHAPTER ONE

'FUN AND GAMES'
PRODUCTION STRATEGIES /
PRODUCTION PROBLEMS

The production history of *Who's Afraid of Virginia Woolf?* has been marked by 'fun and games' of various sorts, from internecine warfare among cast members and production teams to conflicts with external powers over presentation and censorship – which have ranged, in turn, from the sinister to the ludicrous. The extent to which the substance of the play itself lies behind such disputes is variable, but it is surely not merely coincidental that the performative vitriol on stage has so often been mirrored by controversies off. Certainly, in the cases of the opening production and the film version, the frank abrasiveness of Albee's text flew in the face of the prevailing conservatism of Broadway and Hollywood alike, with the respective producers engaging in what, in many respects, were calculated acts of provocation. In both instances, *Virginia Woolf* appeared at the right time and in the right conditions to facilitate a kind of breakthrough: Albee's play, quite beyond the author's intent, took up a vanguard position in the liberalisation of attitudes which took place during the course of the 1960s. In this chapter, I shall examine the circumstances surrounding these productions in some detail, before moving on to outline, more briefly, the major American and British revivals of subsequent decades. Though possessing nothing like the shock value of the earlier versions, these productions have redefined the play in their own, subtler ways, and have often conjured controversies all their own.

WRITING PROCESS, 1961–2

Who's Afraid of Virginia Woolf? is usually regarded as Edward Albee's first 'full-length' play, although he has always denied the validity of that label, stressing that any play should be as long or as short as its author feels it needs to be. The off-Broadway successes of his controversial one-act plays *The Zoo Story*, *The American Dream* and *The Death of Bessie Smith* had already proved his point for him, raising more public and critical interest in 1960 and 1961 than did the work of most of Broadway's established three-act artisans put together. Two other, still shorter, works, *The Sandbox* and *Fam and Yam*, had also appeared in the same period, and though the latter was little more than a satirical sketch, the former is still justifiably seen by Albee as one of his best works, a fifteen-minute jewel worthy of standing alongside Samuel Beckett's similarly distilled shorter works. Given this prolific output of short plays, however, it was perhaps inevitable that expectations were sky-high for Albee's first extended work.

Perhaps conscious of such pressures, Albee allowed *Virginia Woolf* to evolve over time, rather than rushing into writing it. The basic concept had been in his mind at least as early as February 1960, when, following the opening of *The Zoo Story*, he told the *New York Times* that he was planning to write a piece called *The Exorcism*. He mentioned that it might carry the comic subtitle 'Who's Afraid of Virginia Woolf?', a witty graffito he had recently seen in the men's room of a Greenwich Village bar; 'but it's not a funny play', he stressed (Albee 1960). With productions of his various one-act plays taking up much of Albee's attention over the next eighteen months, it was not until the summer of 1961 that he began to flesh out these initial ideas for the play. While vacationing at Water Island, he drafted the first two acts and twenty pages of the third. The remainder of the final act, together with revisions to the first two, was then completed in the spring of 1962 at his apartment in Greenwich Village.

The development of Albee's ideas between these two stages of writing is fairly clearly indicated by the draft scripts archived at New York's Lincoln Center Library for the Performing Arts. Though the final text for the first two acts still stands substantially as it did in the first draft, and thus retains a powerful sense of spontaneity, Albee made various minor adjustments, like replacing some of the easier, cruder abuse (the first draft is liberally sprinkled with such epithets as 'bitch', 'cow' and 'asshole') with more emotionally charged alternatives. At the second stage of writing, he also gave Nick a name, where previously all the character's lines had been attributed simply to 'Dear'. The dialogue itself remained unaffected by this change, since Nick is never actually referred to by name by George and Martha, and Honey persists in calling him 'dear' just as he calls her 'honey'. Yet the effect is nevertheless to make the playscript itself appear more straightforwardly realistic, and less obviously cartoonish or 'absurdist' – thus effecting an important modification in the first impressions formed by his producers, director and actors.

The most significant advance in this second phase of writing, however, was unquestionably the creation of George and Martha's imaginary child, no mention of which appears in the earlier draft material. Albee's 1960 reference to the play as *The Exorcism* indicates that he had always had a purging of some sort in mind for this marriage (and the Latin litany was mentioned in that same early interview), but it was only with the writing of the third act that this idea seems to have found a clear form. Albee then went back and inserted various references to the child into the earlier stages of the script, such as George and Martha's argument preceding Nick and Honey's first entrance: 'Just don't start in on the bit about the kid' (19). (The traces of this particular change are still evident in the text: George's repetition of the line 'All right love . . . whatever love wants' brackets the inserted passage, whereas in the earlier drafts he said this only once.) The relatively late insertion of such details points up the fact that, for Albee, the gesture toward conventional plot mechanics was an afterthought rather than the initial focus of his attention: in the writing, the moment-by-moment ebb and flow of confrontations between characters was always the source of the play's momentum. Interestingly though, if the insertion of the child device is – on one level – a concession to linear plot development, it was also at this stage in the writing that Albee very self-consciously inserted material which would frustrate any attempt to read the play's revelations as presenting a straightforwardly 'true' narrative of the characters' past. Apparently clarifying for himself what the play was doing with the themes of truth and illusion, Albee made other adjustments to the previous acts, such as in the passage where George attempts to recover from Martha's revelations about his 'first novel'. Here, Albee inserted the lines 'True or false? Hunh? I mean, true or false that there ever was such a thing. HA!' (86), thereby rendering far more ambiguous George's next reference to the novel as 'my . . . memory book'. Where in the first draft it seems clear that the novel really was autobiographical (and that his strangling attack on Martha is thus motivated by fury at her revelation of a dark secret), the changes destabilise this reading. The third act exchange in which Martha and George collectively mock Nick's attempts to make sense of their stories then confirms the unresolvability of this issue:

> NICK: Hell, I don't know when you people are lying, or what.
> MARTHA: You're damned right!
> GEORGE: You're not supposed to . . . At any rate . . . My Mommy and
>   Daddy took me [to the Mediterranean] as a college graduation
>   present.
> MARTHA: Nuts!
> NICK: Was this after you killed them?
> [*GEORGE and MARTHA swing around and look at him; there is a brief,
>   ugly pause.*]
> GEORGE [*defiantly*]: Maybe.
> MARTHA: Yeah; maybe not, too.   (*118*)

Interestingly, the first public exposure of material from the play took place well before Albee had written his third act or made the consequent alterations to acts I and II. In the autumn of 1961, Albee consented to be the subject of an extensive interview for a series of programmes called 'Playwrights at Work', which was being prepared by the National Educational Television network. In response to the request for rehearsal footage of work in progress, he offered the first fifteen pages of his then-untitled new script. This opening scene between George and Martha, minus 'the bit about the kid' and leading up to the entrance of – who knew? – was staged by the eventual director of the full premiere, Alan Schneider, who elected to work with actors Peggy Feury and Shepperd Strudwick (later to become the second Broadway George). Albee has not divulged whether or not his subsequent completion of the play benefited from seeing this early scene fleshed out in this way: it proved useful commercially, however, since WNET elected not to broadcast the programme until 15 October 1962, two days after the play's premiere (and the same day that the press reviews appeared). 'This was excellent TV', the New York *Daily News* television critic enthused the next day, noting that 'capital use' was made of 'the charged excitement that attends a controversial but explosively creative drama'. This a mere 24 hours after the same newspaper's theatre critic, John Chapman, had dismissed the play as being 'four characters wide and a cesspool deep' (Chapman 1962a).

PRODUCING THE PREMIERE

If the writing of *Who's Afraid of Virginia Woolf?* had taken time, so too did the process of finding the right circumstances for that first production. With the play finished, Albee initially offered it to Lee Strasberg's Actors Studio, a school with which he had developed close links, despite the apparent gulf between the strictly observed naturalism of Strasberg's 'Method', and the more offbeat, absurdist-inflected approach of Albee's early one-acts. Then at the height of its fame, the Studio was planning to expand its horizons beyond its teaching activities and was looking for a property with which to launch itself as a producing theatre. Albee's play seemed like a good prospect, since the author's status as the much-debated *enfant terrible* of the off-Broadway scene would guarantee public interest in his collaboration with the Studio, while the play itself appeared to be the kind of intense, realist drama at which Method actors excelled. Initially persuaded of the mutual advantages involved in using the Studio's prestige to launch Albee on Broadway, Strasberg proposed to cast Geraldine Page and Eli Wallach as Martha and George, and to have Alan Schneider (also an associate of the Studio) direct. That plan was abandoned, however, when Strasberg capitulated to pressure from his producing colleagues Cheryl Crawford and Roger L. Stevens, who persuaded him that the play was too long, too vulgar, too humourless, and unworthy of the Studio's attentions. Instead, the Studio launched a short-lived Broadway career with a revival of Eugene O'Neill's *Strange Interlude*, which, quite apart from being even longer and vastly less amusing than *Virginia Woolf*, proved to have dated badly since 1928.

Immediately Strasberg backed out, Albee handed the play over to Richard Barr and Clinton Wilder, whose company had handled the off-Broadway productions of his previous plays. Albee now confesses that he would have been happy to see *Virginia Woolf* produced in similar circumstances ('I didn't know whether it should [be on Broadway] or not'), and certainly this was the preference of Alan Schneider, who was still slated to direct. 'I didn't think it had a chance commercially,' Schneider stated in a symposium on the play in 1982, 'I always said, "Don't do it on Broadway"' (quoted McNally 1982: 19). Albee, after all, had no Broadway track record, and in that arena his play would appear unprecedentedly frank in its use of 'strong' language, its character portrayals and its treatment of sexuality. Richard Barr, however, though well aware of the risks, decided that the time was right to try to push Albee on to the 'top rung' of New York's theatrical ladder. Broadway, after all, was then still the only arena in which a new play would be treated seriously enough for elevation to the status of a 'major work'. *Who's Afraid of Virginia Woolf?*

seemed the obvious choice with which to take this next step, and Barr was conscious that it would have been a failure of courage on his part *not* to attempt this, given that the production company he had founded was explicitly dedicated to advancing the cause of a serious American theatre.

Barr was a highly adept producer, but was also far more than a mere exploiter of commercial potential. He had left his partnership in the Broadway firm of Bowden, Barr and Bullock in 1959, having grown increasingly dissatisfied with what he viewed as the company's misplaced priorities. In 1953, for example, they had supported director Joshua Logan in a dispute with playwright William Inge over his play *Picnic*, forcing Inge to make substantial changes to the last act in order to better suit the tastes of Broadway audiences. This kind of treatment was fairly standard for Broadway writers during this period: in 1955, no less a figure than Tennessee Williams was forced into extensive rewrites for *Cat on a Hot Tin Roof* when director Elia Kazan predicted commercial and critical failure without them. Richard Barr, however, believed firmly that if the American theatre was to realise its artistic potential, it needed first and foremost to serve its playwrights. Abandoning, at least temporarily, the commercial rat-race of Broadway, he began producing new plays at smaller, off-Broadway theatres. In 1959 he established Theatre 1960 (the company's title was updated for each subsequent season), and in 1961 he forged what became a seven-year alliance with wealthy producing partner Clinton Wilder. Wilder too had worked on Broadway productions but was more interested in producing quality work at off-Broadway venues such as the Phoenix (where in 1955 he had co-produced a landmark production of Pirandello's *Six Characters In Search of An Author*). Like Barr, he knew that the economics of production were distinctly less cut-throat off-Broadway than on.

Broadway theatre had been hit badly by the inflationary atmosphere of the post-war 'boom' years, as spiralling production costs and falling attendances conspired to drive up ticket prices. Consequently, producers were less willing than ever to take risks on new or unproven material, and during the 1950s many of New York's more adventurous theatremakers chose (or were forced) to work in the low-paid but relatively intimidation-free atmosphere of the emerging off-Broadway scene (which had been granted professional status in 1949 when Actors' Equity permitted its members to work there at a lower weekly pay-rate). Yet, with a few notable exceptions, off-Broadway was at this time a 'library stage', in the sense of mounting either classic revivals or imports of new European plays which had already proved themselves in Paris or London. New work by young American playwrights appeared only rarely, since commercial pressures – though less intense than on Broadway – were nevertheless an increasingly dominant factor in off-Broadway production throughout the 1950s, and producers were simply not prepared to take risks on unknown quantities. Ironically, even Albee had had to 'become European' before finding an American production: his first play, *The Zoo Story*, received its world premiere in German translation in Berlin in 1959, appearing on a double bill with Samuel Beckett's latest piece, *Krapp's Last Tape*. Richard Barr, who had optioned Albee's play as his first independent acquisition, realised that the same pairing might also work in New York: his production opened in January 1960, with Albee's play unexpectedly attracting the bulk of the popular and critical attention (Barr and Wilder responded to public demand by reviving *The Zoo Story* eight times over the next six years). That production also brought Albee to the attention of Alan Schneider, who had directed the American premieres of both *Waiting for Godot* and *Endgame*, and whom Beckett had specified must direct *Krapp*. Although *Zoo Story* was originally directed by Milton Katselas, Schneider was sufficiently impressed by the writing that he offered to direct Albee's next one-act piece, *The American Dream*. What Beckett and subsequently Albee saw in Schneider was an able, hard-working director who was primarily concerned with realising the playwright's vision on the stage with as little interpretative 'spin' as possible from himself. He was the ideal director to assist in Barr's dream of reviving a 'playwright's theatre' on Broadway, and in 1962 he was brought on board from the outset as plans were made to premiere *Virginia Woolf.*

If the decision to produce the play on Broadway was a calculated commercial risk – undertaken out of an admirably idealistic belief in the need to rejuvenate an important theatrical arena which had become creatively moribund – this idealism was also backed up by an unapologetically pragmatic approach to development and marketing. Barr and Wilder, described by Albee as 'the shrewdest producers I have ever met' (Kolin 1988: 29), understood immediately that the play's controversy value, just as much as its artistic virtues, could be exploited to sell tickets. Indeed, it was with the prospect of creating a *succès de scandale* that they persuaded impresario Billy Rose to book the show into the theatre which bore his name. Known as a promoter of musical revues and the creator of the Aquacade (a sort of theatrical version of Busby Berkeley's synchronised can-can swimming), Rose saw Albee's play as a potential hit if its foul-mouthed naughtiness could be turned to marketing advantage (he was particularly fond of George's game 'Hump the Hostess'). A former copywriter, Rose went as far as personally penning newspaper advertisements for the show's low-price previews, appealing directly to secretaries by informing them that they would understand the play even if their bosses did not. Rose was apparently tuned to the same wavelength as the reviewer who later condemned the play as being 'For Dirty-Minded Females Only'.

Rose also, however, vetoed a more ambitious publicity stunt dreamed up by Richard Barr, who suggested opening the play in two different productions simultaneously, on and off-Broadway, with different casts, directors and sets, 'the point being that one of them might get away with it' (quoted McNally 1982: 19). Barr's explanation is disarming but also somewhat disingenuous: financial realities were not such that you could pull such a stunt just to see if one production 'worked' better than the other. This was clearly an attempt to play on the controversy value of the perceived gap between Broadway and off-Broadway standards, perhaps even to taunt Broadway audiences and critics with the more enlightened, intellectual attitudes of the off-Broadway crowd, whom Barr knew would continue to champion the piece even if the headline production folded early. Rose, however, was utterly opposed to this idea, and understandably so, given that it was his theatre which stood to end up looking foolish. Barr was not in a position to bargain with Rose on this point and, in retrospect, Albee is profoundly grateful for the shelving of the plan. It was, he says, 'one of those silly notions. A very, very silly notion.'

Far less silly was the producer's determination to rehearse the play in the actual theatre space where it was to be presented. It was this plan which, according to Barr, had necessitated the use of the Billy Rose in the first place, since this 'was the only theatre available for what we wanted to do: move onto an empty stage to put in our set and lights' (McNally 1982: 19). The theatre was hardly ideal in other respects: besides being located on 41st Street, several blocks south of Broadway's hub around 44th and 45th Streets, its stage was 'considered too large for a straight play and too small for a musical' (Schneider 1986: 312), and would not lend itself easily to the kind of close-up intimacy demanded by Albee's single-set chamber play. Yet the practice of rehearsing on set, greatly favoured by actors and directors, was one of the artist-friendly aspects of off-Broadway production which Barr and Wilder were intent on bringing to Broadway. Their preparedness to make sacrifices to this principle is nowhere clearer than in the fact that, given the union rules governing Broadway production, the use of the theatre itself for rehearsals necessitated the employment of three full-time crew members to sit around doing nothing.

In calculating for such circumstances, Barr and Wilder budgeted the production at $75,000, to be raised by selling share units at $1,500 each. This total was vastly more than what it would have cost to mount a comparable off-Broadway production, but was still cheap for Broadway. In the event, only $55,000 was raised, a sum that included $14,000 invested by Barr and Wilder themselves and $750 from one of the cast members, George Grizzard. The eventual costs of mounting the production, however, totalled less than $47,000. Such economic prudence ensured that the producers made themselves at least partially immune to the familiar Broadway hazard of negative reviews killing the show at birth. The surplus capital meant that they were in a position to let the show run at a loss for some while, thus allowing time for audiences to build up via word-of-mouth should the initial press reception prove unfavourable. In this regard, as in so many others, Barr's planning represented a careful infiltration of off-Broadway production principles into the Broadway arena. Albee, for one, is in no doubt about the importance of this approach to the production's success. As he remarked wryly in a 1967 interview,

> it didn't get the full-blown [Broadway] treatment. The script wasn't changed: none of the actors asked for their parts to be rewritten so they'd be more sympathetic; we didn't have a director who wanted to be terribly creative and change all of the author's lines. No, it wasn't the usual full-blown treatment at all. It was a sneaky little low-budget production. But it managed to have damned good actors and a good director. It was put on pretty much exactly the way I wrote it . . . as I wanted it done. (*Kolin 1988: 83*)

CASTING AND REHEARSALS

The one factor Albee omits here is that the 'damned good actors' were not quite the all-star cast initially intended. All involved knew that, to sell the play on Broadway, the star system would have to be embraced to some degree, and Billy Rose had only consented to lease his theatre on the explicit condition that big names should be involved. In the event, though, only Uta Hagen could lay claim to such status, and even she – despite her reputation as one of America's most distinguished actresses – was making a comeback to the Broadway stage after a self-imposed exile of several years. Despite the best efforts of the producers, the other three cast members were relative unknowns, a factor which indicates just how 'dangerous' appearing in the play was thought to be for established names. Henry Fonda, who was Albee's first choice for George, was not even shown the script by his agent, who simply took it as read that his appearing in the play was out of the question. (According to Alan Schneider, Fonda told him years later that his greatest regret was that 'I never got to play George' [1986: 313].) The first choice for Martha, Geraldine Page, was lost to the production for even more bizarre reasons: despite the Actors Studio having pulled out of producing the play, she was insistent that her mentor and teacher Lee Strasberg be intimately involved. Albee recalls that 'Gerry loved the play and said she wanted to do it very much, but that Lee had to be there at all the rehearsals. And so we said sorry Gerry.' Katherine Hepburn was sent the script, but she turned it down saying she was not good enough for the part. The next choice was Uta Hagen, who with her husband Herbert Berghof ran one of Lee Strasberg's major actor-training competitors, the HB Studio. Four pages into reading the script, Hagen was determined to play Martha, although she had severe personal reservations about working with Alan Schneider.

It was Schneider, however, who proved the key figure in determining the rest of the casting. Various potential Georges had been discussed, from Richard Burton to Robert Flemyng, but none proved appropriate or available. It was somewhat in desperation that Schneider suggested Arthur Hill, a Canadian actor better known in London than New York, whom he remembered seeing on Broadway in James Agee and Tad Mosel's Pulitzer Prize-winning play, *All The Way Home*: 'He didn't seem ideal for us, but he was around fifty, male . . . and available' (Schneider 1986: 314). Albee himself had never heard of Hill, but by this stage he was prepared to take Schneider's recommendation on trust. Schneider also proposed that George Grizzard, one of his favourite actors, with whom he had worked on several previous occasions, be cast as Nick, and Albee agreed despite the fact that Grizzard was not as physically imposing as the 'quarterback' he had envisaged in the role. Melinda Dillon, a Broadway new-comer but something of a protégée of Schneider's, was cast as Honey even though, again, Albee had never heard of her. Only Grizzard put up a serious objection to this final casting decision, on discovering that Dillon was taller than he – a fact which hardly helped in his attempt to envisage himself in the role of a young stud. According to Schneider, it took considerable persuasion to prevent him from quit-ting the production.

Thanks to contractual and financial necessity, the less-than-stellar cast had only three weeks to rehearse a play lasting three-and-a-half hours, prior to the first of ten preview performances. The situation was exacerbated by Arthur Hill's late arrival, following a three-day overshoot on the film he had been making in London. That the pro-duction came together in the frighteningly short time that remained is testament to the skills of all involved, and to the careful prepara-tion of the key figures before rehearsals began: Schneider claims he read the play 'every day for six months', and that on his first meeting with Uta Hagen to discuss the play, she had 'a big notebook contain-ing eighty million questions which she had already answered. Her preparation was terrific' (quoted McNally 1982: 17, 19). Hagen herself adds that the fact of rehearsing on the stage set itself was also of vital importance:

> To start with a play of that length and difficulty *without* the props and scenery, we would have had to rehearse eight weeks longer. To me, this was one of the unique experiences of my entire life in the theatre, start-ing with the things that are food for the play being alive on stage – every little ice cube, every little clinky glass. I found this the most useful circumstance of any production I've ever been in. (*McNally 1982: 10*)

Clearly Barr's and Wilder's commitment to taking off-Broadway's prioritising of play and actors into the Broadway arena paid impor-tant dividends. Even so, the time pressures took their toll. Arthur Hill, whose busy schedule had not allowed him the same preparation period as the others, reportedly lost 10 pounds in the three weeks as a

1. Arthur Hill as George and Uta Hagen as Martha in the original Broadway production, 1962. Note the attention to detail in William Ritman's set.

result of anxiety over learning his lines and moves in time. Although Hill remembers the rehearsals as 'tremendously stimulating' (Spector 1990: 194), Alan Schneider claims that he seemed to need almost constant reassurance and support while developing his role. Schneider also suggests that there was a certain tension between Hagen and Hill owing to their radically different approaches to acting: Hagen used a rigorously psychological approach to exploring Martha's motivations, while Hill – operating more in the British tradition – 'was what Method-trained actors always contemptuously term "a technical actor." Each move, each gesture, came from outside, studied and deliberate' (Schneider 1986: 321).

Schneider's account here, however, is hardly an objective one, since the greatest difficulty during rehearsals was the continuous, underlying tension between Hagen and Schneider himself. The various accounts of the problem conflict somewhat, but it is clear that Hagen had little respect for Schneider from the outset, and stipulated that she would only take the part on the understanding that he would not interfere with her artistic judgement. Schneider believed that her hostility originated with a feud he had had with Herbert Berghof over the Broadway premiere of *Waiting for Godot* in 1956 (Berghof had taken over direction of the production after Schneider pulled out following a débâcle over its preview run in Miami: Berghof publicly accused Schneider of ineptitude; Schneider sued Berghof – unsuccessfully – for stealing his blocking). Hagen insists, however, that her objections were more than merely personal: 'He was wonderful with producers and very often with playwrights,' she has said of Schneider, 'but with actors he was a sadist . . . Those kind of stories were rampant among theatre people. [But] he was never mean to me. He was scared of me' (Spector 1990: 181). Hagen's comments on Schneider's unpopularity with actors are not without foundation: in her autobiography, Colleen Dewhurst (who worked with Schneider on the premiere production of Albee's *Ballad of the Sad Cafe*, and later played Martha in Albee's own 1976 revival of *Virginia Woolf*) makes her own intense dislike for him patently clear. As Albee himself remarks diplomatically in a contribution to Dewhurst's book, 'I do know that Alan occasionally had trouble with strong women' (Dewhurst 1997: 251). To be fair to Schneider, though, there were other actors who adored him: Nancy Kelly, who played Martha on the 1963–4 road tour, remarked simply that 'I'd trust Alan with my life' (Gardner 1963).

Part of the problem between Hagen and Schneider clearly lay in their radically differing approaches to preparation and rehearsal. Hagen's acting and teaching practice was grounded in the Stanislavsky system, which for her meant that preparation for a role must be painstakingly carried out in advance, in order to think oneself into the psyche of the character. She was therefore dismayed when, at her first meeting with Schneider (a five-hour lunch date at Sardi's), he seemed unable to answer any of the questions she had about the play, and confessed to being less well prepared than she. Schneider's apparent lack of readiness, however, reflected his preference for not attempting to answer the play's questions prior to rehearsals. He preferred, instead, to see how the dynamic of the piece would develop on stage with the particular actors involved. For a director committed to exploring the potential of the writer's text rather than imposing his own vision over it, this was an understand-able approach, especially given that this play hinged entirely on the interaction of the four actors and the fluidity of their dialogue: 'I had a terrible time trying to plan the staging ahead of time,' he notes, because 'there were too many imponderables' (Schechner 1965: 146). Schneider's more pragmatic, step-by-step approach meant that he was as dismayed by Hagen as she was by him, perceiving her pre-rehearsal decisions about Martha to be 'totally formed in her mind and not negotiable' (Schneider 1986: 317).

Whatever the rights and wrongs of this dispute, it is clear that Schneider chose discretion as the better part of valour and opted to shape the production *around* Hagen's performance, while allowing her an almost totally free hand in developing her ideas. He always insisted, publicly, that he had immense admiration for her work, and saw very little need to intervene in the development of her performance, since he almost always agreed with her decisions. This approach, however, simply added to Hagen's disrespect for him: 'The best thing Schneider did is that he didn't interfere', she told critic Susan Spector: 'He didn't help. He didn't have any ideas, so obviously I had ideas because he never told me one word' (Spector 1990: 194). Schneider's bowing to Hagen's will also resulted – more importantly – in a premiere production in which the play was perceived as revolving around Martha's dynamic presence, with the other characters acting as foils for her onslaughts. This is not to say that the other actors were ridden over roughshod: as Arthur Hill notes, 'she could be a steam-roller, I imagine, if she feels she's in company where somebody needs to be steam-rolled. [But] George Grizzard and I were certainly not folks who were going to be steam-rolled. I think she knew that' (Spector 1990: 195). Yet the per-formance that emerged was a long way from the four-way ensemble piece which *Virginia Woolf* has become in other incarnations. All the actors realised their parts powerfully, but Uta Hagen, the one genuine 'star' of the production, was indisputably the focus of attention.

2. George Grizzard, Uta Hagen, Arthur Hill in a confrontational moment
from the 1962 production. Note the exact same image reappears with equivalent actors in the film version.

For his part, Albee himself remained largely at a distance from the
day-to-day wrangles of rehearsals, preferring to allow Schneider to
get on with things without feeling the author was breathing down his
neck. By his own admission, Albee was at this stage a relative novice
with regards to the production process, and indeed on that level felt
himself to be learning from Schneider. He too preferred to see how
the piece would develop organically, without imposing solutions in
advance, although this only added further to Hagen's frustrations: 'I
asked Edward, "How do you want to use the child?" and he said "I
don't care. However you want." My questions remained totally unanswered' (Spector 1990: 188). Albee went into the theatre to see rough
versions of each act when they had been mapped out, but made very
few comments on what he saw. His intervention was felt mostly
through the appearance of various judicious cuts in the text, which
reduced the play's running time by an estimated fifteen minutes. In
keeping with Barr and Wilder's playwright-first policy, nobody had
required these cuts from him, despite the play's unusual length.

3. Uta Hagen and Arthur Hill as George and Martha in the 1962 Broadway premiere, with Melinda Dillon as Honey and George Grizzard as Nick.

However, hearing the text played aloud and discussed among the cast clearly helped him arrive at some decisions on fine-tuning. One or two of his changes, moreover, actually saved him some blushes. In the rehearsal script, for example, both George and Nick refer to 'chromozones' without further comment. Someone apparently corrected Albee on his scientific terms, and he chose to make his own error a feature of the text by having Nick point out to George that the word is 'chromosomes'.

Among Albee's more significant changes were the excision of George's farewell speech to Nick and Honey at the end of Act III, which, as Christopher Bigsby observes, was 'a redundant summary of character and action [which] was deleted with some purpose and effect' (Bigsby 1984: 272). Much the same was also true of the biggest cut made during rehearsals: nine pages of dialogue between George and Honey were removed from the beginning of Act III, so that the action moved straight into Martha's 'daddy white mouse' monologue. The abandoned scene, which had somewhat laboriously revealed Honey's decision to blank out her memory of events

at the end of Act II, over-emphasised both her apparent vacuous-
ness and George's cruel dismissiveness. It was effectively substituted
for by the simple addition of a few, more pointed, lines from Honey
to George after her re-entry later in the act: 'I've decided I don't
remember anything . . . and you don't remember anything, either'
(124).

   Albee's changes to the dialogue were complemented by his decision to tone down some of his more explicit stage directions. It is
unclear whether these changes resulted from a discomfort with seeing
them acted out, from objections raised by cast and director (several of
whom expressed reservations about the extent to which the script dictated stage action as well as dialogue), or from a degree of self-censorship motivated by the imminence of the Broadway premiere.
Whatever the cause, however, the final, published script lacks a
number of directions which appear in the rehearsal script. For
example, both George and Martha's 'blue games for the guests' (Act I)
and Martha's attempted seduction of Nick were originally described
in much more graphic physical detail, complete with descriptions of
male hands cupping breasts and even being inserted into Martha's
cleavage. Similarly, Albee elected to delete the third-act directions
suggesting that George should physically brutalise Martha in preparation for the final game of 'bringing up baby' – by pulling her hair,
manhandling her head and slapping her face. One can well imagine
Hagen raising objections to such treatment, but the deletion of these
directions was also in line with Albee's general tendency – in his fine-
tuning of the script – to weed out those words and actions which
seemed casually excessive in their violence rather than pointedly
forceful. The play is much better for these adjustments.

PREMIERE PERFORMANCES

Albee made further minor changes during the ten preview performances, and Schneider also tightened up the staging somewhat.
However, the show that eventually appeared before the opening night

audience was substantially the same one that the first preview audience had seen. As the decision to forgo the usual, pre-Broadway try-outs in New England indicates, there was never any intention of revising the play for the satisfaction of commercial audiences. The producers did not have the money to budget for such a tour anyway, and since regional audiences were thought to be even less open-minded than Broadway audiences, there was no benefit to be gained from going out of town. Instead, the ten previews were scheduled to allow the performers to 'break the play in' before sympathetic spectators: indeed the first five drew their audiences, by invitation only, from the local theatrical community. This was another calculated risk on the part of the producers: as Richard Barr notes, it was precedent-breaking because 'usually you don't want [other actors] anywhere near your show until it's opened and the critics have had their say' (McNally 1982: 9). In this instance, however, it was felt that if anybody was likely to appreciate the special qualities of the play at first sight, it would be other theatre people. Sure enough, the preview audiences began to talk up the production *before* the critics had had their chance to praise or damn it. About four thousand invited guests witnessed the first five performances, and by the time that the five open-access previews gave the general public a first glimpse of the play, word-of-mouth praise and Billy Rose's 'advertisements for secretaries' had ensured that there was barely a ticket to be had, despite the almost complete absence of advance sales a few days previously. The success of Barr and Wilder's preview ploy meant that previews became a regularly-used alternative to try-out tours during the 1960s. As critic Martin Gottfried noted in his 1967 book *A Theater Divided,* 'previews as we know them today were invented' through the precedent set by *Virginia Woolf.* The practice had reintroduced 'a theater for playgoers who were willing to gamble along with the producer', who would opt to see a play at a cheaper rate before they had been told what to think about it. These audiences, Gottfried notes, 'were nowhere to be seen once a production opened. They were new, unrecognized, strange. They were the lost excitement of a living theater' (Gottfried 1967: 53).

The official opening night performance, on Saturday 13 October 1962, was attended by an audience featuring such luminaries as novelist Carson McCullers and director Franco Zeffirelli. Following the success of the previews, there was an expectant 'buzz' among those attending, and Schneider recalls sensing a growing excitement in the auditorium during the play, which climaxed in a sustained standing ovation. Albee himself had spent the evening in his customary standing position at the back of the stalls, pacing back and forth, but refused to go up to the stage in response to the cries of 'Author! Author!' Observers noted that he had seemed shyly diffident throughout the evening. The cast, similarly, opted to avoid the customary celebrations of the first night party, partly because – with the production having opened on a Saturday – there would be no overnight reviews to wait up for. A gathering was held instead at Clinton Wilder's home on the Sunday night, during which Billy Rose took down the breaking reviews in shorthand as they were reported to him over the telephone. Schneider recalls Rose's face 'getting sadder and sadder' as John Chapman's damning *Daily News* review emerged: 'his mouth [was] clamped around a huge cigar which kept drooping further and further earthward' (Schneider 1986: 328). It later emerged, however, that Rose was offering a prize-winning performance of his own. 'He had got some information already', Albee recalls: 'he had some people get some of the reviews and phone him without telling us. Then he withheld those good ones from us. [He was] a very tricky man. He wanted to buy out Barr and Wilder, but they wouldn't sell it to him.' The producers knew as well as Rose that the tabloid condemnations were potentially as beneficial to box-office takings as the more positive reviews from broadsheets like the *New York Times*, which were read out later in the evening. Playwright Doric Wilson, who worked on the show as an unpaid production assistant, sums up the response to the reviews as follows:

> Do you know Noel Coward's play *Design for Living*? Act II starts with a playwright, young playwright who has just opened, and they're reading the reviews that say how dirty, how smutty, and everybody's turning somersaults because they realise that with every 'dirty smutty' that's

another couple of million in the box office. And that's exactly what we
went through at Richard's the next morning [Monday]. Throwing the
papers in the air! Because all it meant was money.

Virginia Woolf 's profile as a controversial play alternately praised
and reviled by the critics secured its survival on Broadway. On
Monday 15 October alone, $13,000 was taken at the box-office in
advance sales (this with the most expensive ticket retailing at $7.50).
The budgeted costs were recouped within five weeks of opening,
and by the time the play had completed its run of 660 performances
on 19 May 1964, it had made a total net profit of over $625,000.
Billy Rose, as the theatre's owner, had earned $8,000 per week for
most of the duration of the run, and Albee himself made over
$150,000. Barr and Wilder had underlined their commitment to the
playwright by making him a partner in their production company,
giving him a 25 per cent stake in the weekly operating profits, as
opposed to the 10 per cent minimum which would have been due to
him under Dramatists' Guild regulations (the show's investors took
the standard 50 per cent). Another, more direct indication of the
producers' determination to channel the show's profits towards their
continued commitment to new playwriting was the establishment in
1964 of the Albarwild (Albee–Barr–Wilder) Playwrights' Unit. This
free, weekly showcase for young writing talent, based at the off-
Broadway Cherry Lane Theatre, was initially financed entirely out of
a share of the profits from *Virginia Woolf.* By Albee's own admission,
the motives here were not 100 per cent charitable: 'it was going to go
to taxes if we didn't figure out something else, so we put it into
experimental theatre' (Kolin 1988: 200). The Playwrights' Unit,
however, became an important link between the commercial theatre
and the writers of the emerging, underground, 'Off-Off-Broadway'
movement. In its ten years of operation, the Unit premiered more
than a hundred new plays by young writers such as John Guare, Sam
Shepard, Lanford Wilson and Mart Crowley. Richard Barr thus
proved to himself and to the world that commercial success on

Broadway could indeed be a means to further artistic ends, not merely an end in itself.

THE FRANCHISE EXPANDS

In the long term, the profitability of *Virginia Woolf*'s original Broadway production was added to considerably by the seemingly endless spin-offs that it generated. In 1963, the original cast performed the play on a mock-up of their set in a CBS recording studio, to create an accurate audio document of their interpretation which was released as a box set of records, and sold unprecedentedly well for a recording of a straight play. Meanwhile, the Broadway production's substitute cast, who were contracted to play only two matinee performances a week, quickly found themselves being invited to play one-night stands at Eastern colleges. This was followed, between September 1963 and May 1964, by a full-scale road company tour, starring Nancy Kelly and Shepperd Strudwick, which moved literally from coast to coast, playing short engagements in major cities all over the nation. Subsequent public demand meant that another road tour kicked off in the autumn of 1964, this time with Vicki Cummings and Kendall Clark in the leads.

The number of different casts which eventually played out variations of Schneider's direction on Ritman's set is worthy of attention in itself. At the time, the idea of having separate matinee and evening casts was unprecedented, and proved to be yet further evidence of Richard Barr's ingenuity in combining canny business practice with artistic interests. His original plan had been for the play to be performed just six times a week, without matinees, in order to save the cast from having to perform the gruelling piece twice on Wednesdays and Saturdays. Billy Rose, however, was unwilling to sacrifice such a large proportion of his potential box-office income. Barr responded by hiring a second cast – an expensive ploy given the tight production budget, but one which would ensure that afternoon audiences saw a performance as fresh and committed as evening patrons would expect. It was, moreover, 'a good public relations angle' (Schneider 1986: 317). 'No other Broadway play, in my recollection, has ever had a complete second cast appearing at the same time', Barr told the *New York Times* when the matinee company opened for business two weeks after the evening premiere. He stressed that 'there has been no resistance by theatregoers' to the scheme: 'in fact, many who saw the play at night want to see the second interpretation' (Gardner 1962). The only person unhappy with this set-up was Uta Hagen, who has always maintained that she was not even consulted over whether she would be willing and able to play all eight performances. She claims she was handed this arrangement as a *fait accompli*, which she person-ally took as an insult, 'a direct reflection on my ability to work, my energy, my strength . . . I played eight times a week for two years in a row without a vacation in *A Streetcar Named Desire*, and *Virginia Woolf* is not as exhausting as that' (McNally 1982: 20). Barr, con-versely, always insisted that Hagen was asked, and that the decision to perform only six times a week was taken for her benefit. Albee offers a possible explanation for this apparent contradiction: 'Uta's *agent* said she couldn't possibly do eight performances. . . . Her agent fucked up.' He is in no doubt, though, that this error proved fortuitous. Likewise Arthur Hill, who found the matinee scheme already in place when he signed up, was very grateful for it: 'Uta felt she could have done both, and by thunder she could have. My feeling was, "Yes, I could go through the lines a second time, but the battery wouldn't really be running"' (Spector 1990: 183).

The first matinee company began rehearsals two days before the senior cast premiered, and featured Shepperd Strudwick as George, alongside the distinguished Canadian actress Kate Reid, who was making her Broadway debut as Martha. Schneider thus found himself back to square one with this version of the play, even as he was making final adjustments on the other. He appeared, however, to relish the challenge. Asked by the *Herald Tribune* whether there was a danger that the matinee cast would be directed with less care, he responded by comparing his situation (somewhat dubiously) with bigamy: 'I've always thought that to be loving and married to two women at the same time is perfectly possible' (Little 1962). Presumably Schneider's two wives would not be expected to dress in the same clothes and move around the same house, as the two *Virginia Woolf* casts were: the basic blocking and use of props was maintained for both versions of the play, so that the stage manager could run them both from the same 'book'. Within those constraints, however, the members of the matinee cast were given as much freedom as possible to develop individual interpretations of their roles, and this is one matter in which Schneider's insistence on developing performances through rehearsal, rather than planning them meticulously beforehand, paid handsome dividends. 'I'm a director who learns the play by doing it,' he explained. Mounting a second version meant that 'I certainly know the play better. I know where the problems are. But because the actors are different, the solutions may be different' (Gardner 1962). This permission to find their own 'solutions' meant that the readings given to the key roles by Reid and Strudwick, and later by Elaine Stritch, Nancy Kelly, Donald Davis, Mercedes McCambridge, Kendall Clark, Vicki Cummings, and so on, all had a freshness and individuality about them that made them distinctly different. In chapter 3, the accounts of these varying interpretations will be discussed in some detail.

The continuing success of the various incarnations of the Broadway production through 1963 and 1964 was mirrored around the world as the licences for foreign productions of *Virginia Woolf* were quickly snapped up. Barr's office received enquiries from Paris, London and Dublin within three days of the Broadway opening. The eventual European premiere, however, was in Stockholm in October 1963, and was directed by Ingmar Bergman for Dramaten, Sweden's national theatre. This was followed in November by the Italian premiere of *Chi Ha Paura di Virginia Woolf?* in Rome. The German version, translated as *Wer Hat Angst vor Virginia Woolf?* by Pinkas Braun – the actor-writer behind the 1959 world premiere of

The Zoo Story – opened shortly afterwards. Israeli and Greek versions appeared in 1964, and in November of that year even Japanese audiences had the chance to experience the play in their own tongue, although – despite good reviews – Takeo Mtsuura's Tokyo production played its brief run to half-empty houses (the public were reportedly puzzled and put off by the play's harsh language). February 1964 saw *Virginia Woolf* arrive in London. The British premiere was yet another incarnation of the original production, and would have appeared earlier had not the decision been taken to wait until Hagen and Hill themselves became available to reprise the roles they had recently surrendered to replacements at the Billy Rose Theatre.

By contrast, of course, the translated productions were all fresh interpretations with their own directors and designers. Yet each nevertheless stuck closely to Albee's intentions. According to the author, for example, Franco Zeffirelli 'essentially copied the New York production' when directing the French premiere in Paris (Stern 1976: 5). Albee recalls finding this version 'fascinating', thanks to very strong performances by Raymond Jerome and Madeleine Robinson as George and Martha. *Qui a peur de Virginia Woolf?* also proved very successful with Parisian audiences, and the run would no doubt have continued well into a second year had it not been suspended after fifty-one weeks because of irreconcilable differences between Jerome and Robinson. For some time before that, the two had reportedly been trading insults on stage which had nothing to do with those Albee had written, ad-libbing personal abuse to such an extent that, by Robinson's admission, the show had 'disintegrated completely from its original text' (Harrison 1965). Jerome claimed that his co-star had taken to beating him with real force across the hands and back on stage, and he finally dropped out of the production amid reports that he was suffering from a nervous breakdown, low blood pressure and shingles. Robinson publicly declared Jerome a clown, and accused him of trying to steal the show from her. Jerome sued for libel. Not to be outdone, Robinson attended the opening night of a production Jerome had directed, *Don Juan in Hell*, and hissed and booed the actors during the performance. The international press had great entertainment with the 'life imitating art' theme, but the whole experience was clearly very traumatic for those involved: with the closing of the production, Robinson announced that she was giving up acting. Thankfully, the French fiasco remains by far the most extreme of the various reported disputes between *Virginia Woolf* cast members.

CENSORSHIP

Who's Afraid of Virginia Woolf? was presented with the New York Drama Critics' Circle Award for Best Play of 1962, and this was swiftly followed by the Outer Critics' Circle Award, five Tony awards (best play, best director, best production, best male lead, best female lead), and a similar sweep of the *Variety* critics' poll (best play, best director, best male lead, best female lead, and Melinda Dillon as 'most promising actress'). Despite the play's mounting celebrity, however, there continued to be influential figures who vehemently disapproved of it. This became evident publicly when the Trustees of Columbia University bucked the awards trend by rejecting the recommendation of their advisory drama panel and refusing to present Albee with the 1963 Pulitzer Prize for Drama. The distinguished panel members, John Gassner and John Mason Brown, promptly resigned in protest, with the result that no prize was awarded that year. Albee says he later learned that, of the eight trustees who outvoted their seven colleagues so as to overturn the recommendation, four had neither read nor seen his play. He claims, however, that the rejection did not bother him greatly (he has won three Pulitzers since). More distressing were the various attempts of local authorities to censor the play when it began touring – attempts which vindicated Richard Barr's decision not to risk regional try-outs prior to the New York opening.

The first trouble came during the very first stop-over for the national road company, in September 1963, in Boston, Massachusetts, a city well known as one of the favoured locations for pre-Broadway performances, but even better known as a wellspring of American puritanism. The head of the city's licensing division, Richard J. Sinnott, took it upon himself to expose the relative permissiveness of the New York authorities by refusing to permit the production to run without cuts. 'I feel it would be a mortal sin to sit back and do nothing while this cesspool backs up', he told the *Boston Herald*, after seeing the opening performance. Sinnott demanded that a dozen 'abuses of the Lord's name' be removed from the script, on the grounds that 'no matter how sophisticated society may think it has become, the ten commandments are much older than that society. The first commandment is repeatedly abused throughout this production.' There was an irony involved here beyond Sinnott's biblical ignorance (the injunction against taking the Lord's name in vain is actually the third commandment). Albee, who wanted *Virginia Woolf* taken seriously, had sought actively to evade the possibility that he might stir up controversy simply over the play's language, and had edited it to remove several uses of the word 'fuck' prior to the Broadway opening – this despite Barr's offer to 'take one "fuck" uptown' (Harris 1994: 88). Most of the complaints in New York had therefore been over the general, frank vulgarity of the play's language, rather than its use of specific words. Certainly Albee's liberal use of the names 'God' and 'Jesus' was not considered particularly reprehensible: such profanity had been a familiar feature of Broadway plays since the 1920s, and had no doubt also been heard in Boston try-outs before this. Yet Sinnott was now choosing to make an issue of this and nothing else. Though he mentioned 'at least fifty other questionable remarks and epithets' in his letter to the manager of the Colonial Theatre, he was willing to concede that these, at least, 'could be argued [to be] in keeping with the context of the play' (*Boston Herald* 1963). But he threatened a suspension of the play's three-week run if the references to God were not removed.

There were, of course, protests about freedom of speech from some sections of the Boston media and from the American Civil Liberties Union, but the play's producers wisely opted not to add any more fuel to this particular fire. Consenting to the required cuts, they noted in a press release that these 'did not seriously affect the artistic integrity of the work' (*Variety* 1963). Albee himself has always regarded expletives as 'useful exclamation points in writing dialogue', but stresses that they 'really don't have any meaning that relates to much of anything' (Kolin 1988: 15). Playing up to the absurdity of the situation in Boston, he facetiously asked if he could replace the play's opening line, 'Jesus H. Christ', with the alternative, 'Mary H. Magdalene', and was delighted to discover that this was acceptable. The first time she performed the altered script, however, Nancy Kelly momentarily forgot herself, bursting on stage with 'Jesus H. Magdalene!' Sinnott chose to let that one ride.

Thankfully, this farce was not repeated at other stops on the national tour, although minor cuts were requested by various local licencing departments, and the projected dates in St. Paul, Minnesota, had to be cancelled when the city refused to grant the play a license at all. A few local critics would attack the play as dirty and scurrilous almost everywhere it appeared, but they only succeeded in playing into Barr's hands: he and his regional associates began openly to exploit such controversy by using it as an advertising tool. During the dates in Chicago, for instance (February–April 1964), newspaper advertisements were taken out quoting both positive and negative reviews from the city's press, as a means of demonstrating its significance as a cultural event: 'Roger Dettmer says: "I urge all who are adult and unsheltered to see it" . . . And Claudia Cassidy says: "It is . . . as revoltingly dull as the maudlin drunks who inhabit it." . . . No true theatre goer in Chicago can afford to miss this opportunity to see Albee's play. You have five more weeks.' Increasingly, a city's ability to appreciate *Virginia Woolf* became an indicator of its social sophistication, an opportunity to prove itself more enlightened than benighted Boston.

This ripple effect did not, however, stretch as far as South Africa, where – simultaneously with the Boston débâcle – the play's first foreign production also ran foul of the moral indignation of local authorities. Albee, whose definition of obscenity was somewhat more broad-sighted than those of his critics, had agreed to license the play in South Africa only if the conventions of apartheid were suspended and all races were permitted to attend the theatre unsegregated. In practice, though, the ticket prices created economic apartheid even if the social divide was notionally inoperable. During the play's September dates in Port Elizabeth only 62 of the 3,000 people who saw it were non-white. This, however, did not deter white pressure groups from picketing the theatre on the grounds that the play was too obscene to be viewed by impressionable blacks. When the production transferred to Johannesburg in October, it was promptly banned by Interior Minister Jan de Klerk for the offence it caused to religious convictions.

Quite the silliest of the various censorship rows was that stoked up by the Lord Chamberlain prior to the British opening. At this point the Lord Chamberlain's office still held the right to censor stage plays for any reason it saw fit, at Her Majesty's pleasure. In April 1963, a full ten months before the London opening, he issued a long list of cuts and changes to the script which would be necessary before British audiences could see the play. Donald Albery, owner of the Piccadilly Theatre, where *Virginia Woolf* was scheduled to appear, wrote to Barr asking whether or not they should 'attempt to get publicity for the play by saying the Lord Chamberlain has requested no less than 67 alterations to this prize-winning play which virtually amounts to its banning as the author does not feel able to comply'.[1] Since this letter was written before the author knew of these requests, it is clear that Albery's primary concern here was publicity rather than freedom of expression; indeed he himself had requested that from ten to fifteen minutes be cut from the play simply because London audiences are 'not accustomed to finishing late, as you do in New York'.[2] That request, however, was rejected, even as Albee looked for ways to appease the Lord Chamberlain. In a letter dated 3 November he agreed to amend 'bugger' to 'bastard'; 'personal screwing machine' to 'either "a personal propagating machine" [as suggested by the censor] or "a personal sex machine"'; 'screw to their hearts' content' to 'do themselves to their hearts' content', and – most bizarrely of all – 'screw baby' to 'hump baby'.[3] Among a number of other changes, he also agreed to render the stage directions for Martha's seduction of Nick 'inoffensive'. ('You are warned', the Lord Chamberlain had written rather mysteriously, 'that the "business" must be limited to normal embracing.')[4] Albee drew the line at the suggestion that he should substitute every reference to 'Jesus' with 'Cheese' (or in one case 'Cheese God'). Yet the Lord Chamberlain refused to budge on this point, and in early February, with the opening fast approaching, Albee finally consented to use 'Cheese' – presumably hoping that if the actors spoke the syllable with sufficient expression, the audience would not even notice the substitution. He requested only that the play's opening 'Jesus H. Christ' outburst be retained, on the grounds that 'it is not in any way meant as blasphemy and does not refer to the Deity but to a member of the Faculty'.[5]

The Lord Chamberlain accepted this explanation with a typical absence of irony, but refused point blank to permit George's references to male genitalia to stay intact: 'they will allow the word "privacies" where the word "scrotum" is at present used', Donald Albery informed Richard Barr on 5 February 'and the word "bowel" instead of "ball"'.[6] Understandably, the notion of Martha being described as her father's 'right bowel' did not appeal, and Schneider credits Albee with the solution (though Albee himself does not recall it): 'Edward suddenly remembered an old Southern expression, "right bawl," meaning a good cry, which someone in his family had used. He would change the entire meaning of the line from "right ball" to "right bawl". To our collective delight, the Lord Chamberlain accepted' (Schneider 1986: 322). Yet no such rhyme seemed available for 'scrotum': Uta Hagen recalls Arthur Hill getting out the line 'the underside of his privacies' on the first night in London, and then refusing ever to say it again. In typically inconsistent manner, the Lord Chamberlain did not try to enforce the point. 'Out of a number of "Jesus Christs" we were allowed three,' Hagen recalls: 'I thought it was wonderful that we were allowed some and not others. We were allowed to say "hump the hostess" because "hump" is in Shakespeare. We were not allowed to say "screw you" because that was dirty' (McNally 1982: 14). 'It was ludicrous,' Albee recalls of the whole affair: 'it was theatre of the absurd.'

ADAPTING THE PLAY TO THE SCREEN

Though the publicity surrounding the Boston and London disputes proved more than a little embarrassing to the censors in question, and contributed to the long-term demise of stage censorship in those cities (the Lord Chamberlain's office was finally abolished in 1968), these were essentially storms in teacups. In terms of breaking down the barriers of censorship, the play's greatest impact was felt as a result of its transformation into a movie. Where theatre censorship chiefly consisted of petty tinkering with productions which were ready to go up, in Hollywood pre-production censorship was still in operation in the early 1960s. None of the major studios would dare to flout the 'Production Code', which issued guidelines *before the fact* as to what could and could not be said or done in an American movie intended for general distribution. The advantage of this system for film-makers was clear: in terms of dialogue, for example, it was far easier to alter a screenplay before shooting than to alter offending footage using reshoots and the conspicuous dubbing over of voices.

Albee was well aware of this system when he signed away the film rights to Warner Brothers in March 1964, accepting a cool 60 per cent of the $500,000 fee while sacrificing any say in how the film was made. He must have fully expected that Hollywood would bowdlerise his play as mercilessly as it had the dramas of Tennessee Williams, but he chose – understandably enough – to take the money and run. Not every day is a writer offered the kind of financial security afforded by a deal of this scale. What Albee could not have anticipated, however, was that a unique conjunction of film-making talent and of contextual circumstances would contrive to result in a movie which broke with precedent in numerous ways. Thanks largely to the sheer bloody-mindedness of its makers, Warner Brothers' version of *Who's Afraid of Virginia Woolf?* rewrote the rulebook of Hollywood convention, much as the stage play had done previously for Broadway. In so doing, it propelled on to mainstream cinema screens events and dialogue which had never previously been seen or heard in America outside art houses, and became directly responsible for the demise of the old Production Code and the advent of the film classification scheme familiar today.

The Production Code Administration (PCA) seems to have sensed its nemesis at a distance, opening a file on *Virginia Woolf* on 15 October 1962, the day that the first reviews of the Broadway premiere hit the streets. Though many assumed that the play would be unfilmable because of its controversial content, except perhaps as a non-commercial art house film which would therefore operate beyond the PCA's jurisdiction, the PCA (like Billy Rose and others before them) clearly recognised its commercial potential. So too did Gregory Peck, who wired Barr on behalf of Universal Studios to enquire about film rights as early as 17 October. However, it was Jack Warner, chief executive of the Warner Brothers studio, who personally secured an option on the play, having seen and adored the stage production. Since Warner Brothers was the only major Hollywood studio not to have a subsidiary arm specialising in art house projects, this also ensured that the Production Code would have to be applied. By March 1963, Warner was already in correspondence with PCA director Geoffrey M. Shurlock, asking him for comment on potential problems with transferring the play to the screen. Shurlock was unambiguous: to earn a Code Seal, the studio would have to 'remove all the profanity and the very blunt sexual references' (Leff 1980: 42).

He listed eighty-three page references and hundreds of words and phrases which would need revision or deletion. Warner Brothers responded by trying to persuade Albee himself to work up a screenplay, and wrote to his agent with a transparent attempt at ego flattery: 'Albee is sufficiently inventive and creative to substitute potent and pungent dialogue that could prove highly effective, even though possibly reducing the "shock" impact of this highly regarded play' (Leff 1980: 42). Unsurprisingly, Albee was not interested in such an exercise, and he must have raised an eyebrow when, after a year of further considerations, Warners picked up their option and handed over the fee.

That the expected butchering of the play did not take place is thanks largely to Jack Warner's appointment of Ernest Lehman as screenwriter and producer. A Hollywood veteran whose previous credits ranged from Hitchcock's *North by Northwest* to *The Sound of Music*, Lehman was initially sceptical about the project since, as a great admirer of the play, he did not want to be party to a screen version which failed to do it justice. However, since Warner insisted that he was the only man for the job, he eventually consented on the explicit condition that he had a free hand to select the cast, director and key production staff for himself. Warner agreed, retaining only the right to approve Lehman's choices. That left Lehman in the position of producing a film which he had not the first idea how to make. Standard Hollywood practice in adapting Broadway plays was to follow the principle of 'opening out' the action by showing events which are only reported in the original dialogue. This was partly to overcome the visually static quality of the stage, and partly because run-of-the-mill dramas frequently benefited from the transposition of laborious expository dialogue into continuous action. With *Virginia Woolf*, however, as Lehman realised, the dialogue *was* the action. The play relied less on the exposition or development of a narrative than on the claustrophobic intensity of the drunken, late-night encounter in George and Martha's living-room:

I was determined that this should not be done as a story about a woman named Martha, who is married to a professor of history named George, and we meet them one day, and two weeks later, Nick and Honey arrive in town, and there's a faculty party, and Martha and George meet them there and invite them over, and after a terrible evening, something happens, and after twenty minutes we dissolve to a classroom with George teaching history. I was *not* going to try to find a story *based* on *Who's Afraid of Virginia Woolf?* I felt that all those who said it can't be done as a film really meant that it can't be done unless you *do* it as a film. (*Newquist 1966: 88*)

Lehman began to think the unthinkable, wondering if he could get away with filming the play almost as it stood. After all, since Albee's dialogue was clearly dramatic, in and of itself, why should his scenario necessarily have to be 'opened out'? Lehman began work on a screenplay which would leave most of the action centred in George and Martha's house, while also reducing the three-hours-plus of Albee's play to a commercially practicable length of around two hours. Mindful of censorship, he substituted phrases such as 'oh my God' for 'Jesus Christ', 'hop the hostess' for 'hump the hostess', and so forth, but Jack Warner was disturbed to discover that numerous curse words of the 'goddamn' and 'sonofabitch' variety remained intact. Any of these would place the film beyond the pale of the Production Code.

Meanwhile, *Virginia Woolf*'s status as a major commercial project was underlined further by the signing up of star actors. Albee's pre-ferred casting choices were Bette Davis and James Mason – a pairing which would have resulted in Bette Davis talking about herself in the opening scene: 'wouldn't that have been wonderful? She would have done her Bette Davis imitation!' Ernest Lehman, however, decided fairly early on that he wanted Elizabeth Taylor for Martha. Like everyone else, he was aware that at 33 Taylor was too young for the part of a 52-year-old, but 'she kept coming back to my mind – there was something very exciting about the thought of Elizabeth Taylor playing this role' (Newquist 1966: 89). Lehman's canny commercial sense told him that the very prospect of casting her so radically against type would stir up audience interest in the project. With the aid of wigs and make-up, Taylor could be made to look about 45, and the use of black and white film could impose a starkness on her features which would cancel out the radiance of Technicolor in which audiences were used to seeing her. When Lehman sent Taylor a copy of Albee's play, she was greatly struck by it, but was not sure she could do it. However, her partner Richard Burton persuaded her to take the role if only 'to stop everyone else from playing it. I don't want any other actress to do it. It's too good a part' (Newquist 1966: 89). Burton was also surely aware that with Taylor on board it was only a matter of time before he was offered the part of George. Other names like Jack Lemmon and Henry Fonda were tossed around by the producers, but with Taylor and Burton at this time the most gossiped-about couple in America, it made sound commercial sense to cast them tearing strips off each other.

Taylor and Burton quickly made their influence felt by strongly advocating the appointment of Mike Nichols as director. Nichols had made his name directing Broadway comedies such as Neil Simon's *The Odd Couple* and *Barefoot in the Park*, but had never before shot a movie. Yet the support of the stars, combined with the 1960s Hollywood trend of ditching industry stalwarts in favour of 'hip' young talents who were thought to be more in tune with the tastes of the movie-going public, resulted in Nichols being given almost total artistic control over the film. He, like Lehman, wanted to shoot a gritty black and white rendering of the play, but was aware that this was considered uncommercial and 'arty', and was prepared to have to fight for his preferences. On his arrival in Hollywood, 'I girded myself for a big battle with Jack Warner over things I didn't want, like Panavision and Technicolor. To my astonishment he agreed – we got every single thing we asked for' (Jennings 1965). Warner clearly knew that times were changing.

Nichols had not made a film before, but he knew theatre, and he understood that a successful translation of *Virginia Woolf* to the screen would have to be achieved not by 'turning it into a movie', but by utilising movie techniques to create a cinematic equivalent for the intensity of its impact on stage. He and Lehman sat down with the working screenplay and promptly discarded almost all the latter's half-hearted attempts at 'opening out' Albee's text. The action would stay in and around Martha and George's home, in the present moment, without scenic diversions or 'explanatory' flashbacks. The one major alteration which made it into the eventual shooting script was Lehman's decision to transplant a section of Act II to a deserted roadhouse, which was retained partly because it allowed for a sub-stantial folding of time (necessary in cutting the play's length down), and partly because both director and producer felt that such a shift of scene was necessary dramatically. 'One of the things that bothered me in the play was that Nick and Honey hung around there all night', Lehman commented later: 'Why don't they go home? What are they taking all this guff for?' (Lehman 1976: 46). By opting to have them leave the house, only to be sidetracked at the roadhouse and drawn back to George and Martha's for the final act, Lehman and Nichols felt they were actually improving on Albee's scenario. Others were less convinced, however: on the film's release, *New York Times* critic Stanley Kauffmann dismissed the roadhouse sequence as 'a patently forced move for visual variety', while praising the film-makers for their restraint elsewhere (Kauffmann 1966c).

Nichols' insistence on keeping most of the action within and around the house was justified visually by his determination to achieve a quasi-documentary feel for the film. The 'stageyness' which so often results when a film makes extended use of a single location could be overcome, he believed, by exploiting the sense of edgy rest-lessness evoked by *cinéma vérité* shooting (originally a side effect of the camera operator's need to improvise visual composition on the spot). Following a recent trend among black-and-white film-makers, Nichols sought to mimic the fluid motion and intrusive proximity of the documentary camera as a conscious stylistic choice. The notion of shooting in confined, 'real-life' locations provided Nichols with an appropriate means of bringing the cinema audience *into* George and Martha's intimate, delusory world (as opposed to trying to open that world *out* for the viewer). Ironically, though, Nichols' decision to reproduce 'lo-fi' visuals as part of the film's aesthetic entailed breaking almost every rule in Hollywood's book, so much so that – quite unlike *cinéma vérité* itself – it became extremely expensive to film.

A short location shoot was arranged for filming exterior scenes at Smith College, Vermont. All of the film's interiors, however, were shot on Warner Brothers sound stages in Hollywood. Somewhat perversely, Nichols deliberately deprived himself of most of the advantages afforded by studio surroundings, and had the production designer, Richard Sylbert, build George and Martha's home with such a level of realism that the dimensions were those of an actual house, and the walls did not open out. The camera was thus confined within the rooms with the actors, exactly as if it were a documentary shoot. Moreover, the 'authenticity' of the rooms (designed by Sylbert after fact-finding visits to no less than eighteen college campuses) extended to the point of using warped floorboards underfoot, which precluded the use of conventional standing studio cameras. All of this might have infuriated any director of photography other than Haskell Wexler, who was best known for his cinematography for documentaries and location-shot narrative films like Elia Kazan's *America America* (1963). Wexler arranged the studio lighting so as to approximate the feel of the 'available light' he would normally use on location, and made extensive use of a handheld camera to follow the actors around the confined spaces. Wexler allowed for the movement of other, larger cameras by laying down temporary tracks on the floorboards, but he also invented a method for the handheld camera to mimic a conventional dolly camera by designing a new camera-cart. By building an upright aluminium frame which could be pushed about like a wheelchair, Wexler was able to suspend a small platform just half an inch above floor height. This allowed the camera operator to sit or stand while being wheeled around the floor, and to step off the platform and begin walking without breaking the fluidity of a shot.

The unconventionality of the shoot extended to such tricks as Wexler – at Nichols' behest – deliberately over-exposing the film on George and Martha's initial entrance to their home, so as to create the sense of them being half-blinded when the lights are flicked on, after being outside in the dark for so long. Yet this device, like all the others, was employed with the aim of creating a sense of intensified realism, similar to that suggested by the play itself, rather than to show off ingenuity for its own sake. As Herb Lightman commented in *American Cinematographer*, 'there are none of the self-consciously arty pogo-stick convulsions affected by certain misguided *nouvelle vague* types' (Lightman 1966: 532). Some observers assumed that the 'marvelously sensitive' camera work – 'like the play itself, its supreme virtue is its intelligence' (Callenbach 1966: 47) – was entirely attributable to Wexler's experience, but Wexler himself was the first to stress that he had simply provided the technical know-how, and that it was Nichols, as first-time director, who had masterminded the look of the film. Like the young Orson Welles, working on *Citizen Kane* twenty-five years previously, Nichols was thrilled by the new box of creative tricks he found at his disposal, and was not afraid to use them. Also like Welles, though, he was not about to forget the fundamental importance of the actors themselves. Unlike most films, which are made in short bursts with the actors learning their lines from scene to scene, *Virginia Woolf* was rehearsed on set for a full three weeks before shooting began. As a result, the actors could be relied on to play out whole sequences as the cameras moved around them, seeking to capture the intensity of their encounters. Still photographs taken on set demonstrate that all four actors would play the scenes for broke even when some of them were not actually in camera-shot. 'I really believe in another ten days we could have taken the play on the road', Elizabeth Taylor told the *New York Times*: 'I've never before rehearsed something straight through on an actual set and blocked it out, the way we did for three weeks with Mike Nichols' (Thompson 1965). There is a striking similarity here with Uta Hagen's comments about the advantages of rehearsing on the Broadway set.

CONFRONTING THE CENSORS

Who's Afraid of Virginia Woolf? today remains an exemplar for the translation to film of intense, theatrical confrontations, albeit one which is learned from all too infrequently. In the shorter term, though, Nichols' most significant decision as director was his simple refusal to accede to Jack Warner's demand that they shoot 'protection footage' for moments in the film which might be subject to censorship when viewed by the PCA. That is, no duplicate footage with toned-down language was shot as back-up, in case cuts were demanded in the more 'frank' exchanges of dialogue. Nichols explained that his refusal to comply with such conventions was motivated as much by ethics as by aesthetics. 'Disguising profanity with clean but suggestive phrases is really dirtier', he told *Life* magazine when the film was released: 'echoes of wild talk, it seems to me, are deliberately titillating. People . . . say certain things to each other that we all have heard, [so we should] let those things take their place and then go back into proportion. We feel the language in *Woolf* is essential to the fabric; it reveals who the people are and how they live' (Thompson 1966: 92).

The problem for Jack Warner, however, was that Nichols' stand left him in an impossible situation. The studio had budgeted the production at $7.5 million, a figure which at that time made it the most expensive non-spectacle movie in history, and that was before the three-week overshoot – at a further $70,000 per day – had been taken into account. The movie *had* to be released and advertised with the full commercial push if it was to retrieve that money and turn any kind of profit, but the movie Nichols presented to Warner was one which the Production Code Administration could not approve – and had *said* they could not approve as far back as March 1963. After seeing a copy of the shooting script, PCA head Geoffrey Shurlock wrote to Warner in October 1965 to stress again that it could not be approved in that form, but by then the film was mostly 'in the can', with Nichols ignoring Warner's pleas for compromise options. On 2

May 1966, the PCA finally saw the completed film, and Shurlock again rejected it as unacceptable for a Code Seal. Yet he also took the bizarre step of urging Warner to appeal against his decision 'in the hope that [the Review] Board would see fit to give this picture an exemption' (quoted Leff 1980: 46). Clearly, although his own hands were tied by the antiquated stipulations of the Code he was employed to enforce (little modified since its inception in 1930), Shurlock recognised the film's artistic merits and believed that it deserved to be seen.

In such circumstances, it was inevitable that something in the system had to give, and Jack Warner began to apply his own considerable weight to this task by letting it be known that Warners would distribute the film to cinemas accompanied by the stipulation that no one under age eighteen should be permitted to see it 'unless accompanied by his parent'. By thus making his own arrangements to protect the innocent, Warner was implicitly threatening to release the film with or without a Code Seal. To do so would be to take the studio outside the patronage of the Motion Picture Association of America, but at this time the beleaguered MPAA probably had more to lose from such a move than did Warner Brothers. Moreover, the 'parental guidance' tag was a provocation in itself, a unilateral imposition of the kind of film classification which the industry as a whole had been resisting for years. Most studio bosses feared losing revenue if sections of the audience were excluded, not to mention the nightmare of red tape which was expected to follow if films began to acknowledge 'adult' content (since different states were thought likely to enact different censorship laws according to taste). In the eyes of many, then, Warner was threatening to open Pandora's Box in order to release this film.

If leverage was being applied, it was given further impetus by the unexpected decision of the National Catholic Office for Motion Pictures (NCOMP), formerly known as the Legion of Decency, to approve the film with an A-4 rating: 'morally unobjectionable for adults, with reservations' (the same rating given to other so-called

'think films' like Fellini's *8½* and *La Dolce Vita*). This was a coup for
Warner Brothers not only because it implicitly supported their own
classification of the film as being intended for adult audiences while
still being decent and responsible, but also because it saved the studio
from another potential confrontation. The approval or disapproval of
'the Legion', as it was still generally known, was thought to carry great
weight with the 'decent' American public, and anticipations of their
reactions often influenced Hollywood producers in deciding what
they could include in a film. Nudity on screen, for example, had
always been unacceptable to the Legion, and would be likely to earn
an offending film a C categorisation, for 'Condemned'. The rarity of
C ratings (Tennessee Williams' *Baby Doll* famously earned one in
1956) was indicative of the Legion's effectiveness as a pre-production
deterrent to 'indecency', but given the uncompromising attitude
taken by Lehman and Nichols with *Virginia Woolf,* there was considerable concern that it would be condemned, if only for its retention
of many of Albee's 'blasphemous' curse words.

The film would, in fact, have been condemned if the traditionalist
group which had been vetting films for NCOMP until 1965 had had
their way. In that year, however, the liberalisation of the organisation
was demonstrated by the decision to counterweight what one executive called the 'little old ladies in tennis shoes' with a new group of
'consultants': film teachers and other professionals who were more
likely to appreciate the artistic merits of serious, adult-oriented
material. The consultants' votes were sufficient to earn the film an
A-4 rating, the associated 'reservations' being – of course – to do with
the film's language: 'I must say I would not like to see the Lord's name
become the easy recourse of a scriptwriter', noted one, 'yet I feel very
strongly that at this time an arbitrary blanket pronouncement regarding language by the Church would do nothing but assure its critics of
a general lack of perception on the Church's part of the values of the
film. There is something being said here which is quite valid and, in
its own terms, very moral' (Thompson 1966: 96). The A-4 judgement applied to the film as an artistic whole, and no cuts were asked

for. Perhaps most significantly though, NCOMP's executive secretary, Monsignor Thomas F. Little, indicated the office's approval of Warners' voluntary classification of *Virginia Woolf* as a film for adults only, and hinted that further relaxation in its own categories might follow if the industry adopted such practices more widely.

As Hollywood's self-censorship body, the MPAA now found itself in the bizarre position of appearing to be more conservative than the guardians of morality it had been established to appease. Geoffrey Shurlock, in particular, must have appreciated the irony: his strict imposition of the Production Code in relation to *Virginia Woolf* was in part a result of the fact that, when he had last tried to interpret it more loosely, in relation to Billy Wilder's *Kiss Me Stupid* in 1964, NCOMP had responded by condemning it. Now, in June 1966, as a result of actions by NCOMP and by Warner Brothers, the MPAA's Review Board found itself with the choice of either denying a Code Seal to a $7.5 million property approved even by the former Legion of Decency, or granting a Code Seal by exempting it from the normal rules. The former option would make them look foolish, the latter would concede ground to the principle that artistic merit could counterweight standards of morality, and would be the thin end of the wedge for the full introduction of classification. An exemption was eventually granted on the grounds that *Virginia Woolf* was a 'superior picture', and on the condition that two 'minor' deletions were made in the soundtrack. Though MPAA chairman Jack Valenti attempted to stress that the film's exemption was *only* that, and should not be regarded as precedent-setting, it was a mere ten days later that he proposed the adoption of a revised Production Code to a conference of three hundred studio executives and film-makers. His revisions, moreover, proved to be an unworkable stop-gap. Within two years of the premiere of *Virginia Woolf*, further legal wranglings resulted in the advent of industry-wide motion picture classification.

The two 'sexual epithets' which Warners dutifully removed from *Virginia Woolf*'s soundtrack were 'frigging', which was simply blanked out, since it was delivered with the speaker's back to camera, and Martha's exclamation of 'Screw you!' as George opens the door to Nick and Honey. Taylor's words were dubbed over as 'Goddamn you!' by a studio voice impersonator – an awkward glitch still visible in the film. Somewhat bizarrely, though, George's remark 'screw baby' was left intact in Act III, thereby raising the question as to whether, in Martha's case, it was the word itself or the violence of the sentiment which was being objected to. It is difficult to avoid the conclusion that the real sticking-point for the moral guardians of the 1960s was that it should be a woman who expressed herself in this way.

For his part, Albee was initially delighted with the film when it was screened for him in June 1966. 'It was an extraordinary relief,' he told the *New York Post*: 'I kept getting reports about terrible things happening to it . . . and now it turns out nothing's been changed except for a couple of phrases that apparently were too strong for them' (Herridge). Like many of the critics, however, Albee expressed reservations about the decision to relocate parts of Act II in a roadhouse: 'the intimacy is destroyed . . . It's the one time it looks like a filmed stage play.' He also noted 'a couple of oversimplifications' resulting from the trimming of the script, and in subsequent years, having overcome his initial relief and surprise, Albee pronounced his dissatisfaction over these points more forcibly. He objects, in particular, to the almost total removal of the historical–political dimension of the play, and to what he feels to be a de-intellectualisation of the characters. George, for example, is permitted far less reflection on history, biology, war, and genetics, while Martha's language is stripped of her more obviously 'clever' lines, so that she is no longer capable of bandying language on the same level as her husband. There is, for example, no trace of such wonderful retorts as 'ABSTRUSE! In the sense of recondite. Don't you tell me words' (44). 'Whenever something occurs in the play on both an emotional and an intellectual level', Albee has commented, 'I find in the film that only the emotional aspect shows through' (Kolin 1988: 51). One other factor Albee was particularly unimpressed with was the choice of musical score. The single most miscalculated element of the film, it provides saccharine strings which artificially guide emotional responses at pivotal moments: 'I saw the rough cut before they put the music in and it was a much better film. Much better. Where did this orchestra come from?'

If Albee's feelings about the film were mixed, the public and critical response was almost unanimously positive. The play's transition from stage to screen seemed only to enhance its reputation: Ernest Callenbach, in his review for *Film Quarterly*, hailed this as not merely 'among the few filmed plays that are also good films', but as 'the best American film of the last several years' (Callenbach 1966: 46). With *Virginia Woolf* already having acquired near-classic status as a play, reviewers were not about to embarrass themselves by complaining too much about the film's morals or lack thereof, and indeed the most consistent complaint about the picture was that the presence of Burton and Taylor distracted attention from a proper appreciation of Albee's script. Callenbach's response was typical, noting that while 'stage audiences have sometimes found the play literally unbearable', the film provides an 'emotional escape hatch' in the shape of its stars: 'we can always reflect comfortably that they are, after all, that famous pair, carrying on' (48). Such objections, of course, disregarded the fact that the film's appeal to mass audiences was largely dependent on its stars. Yet what really surprised commentators was that the 'masses' proved more enthusiastic about the film, and considerably less shocked and disgusted, than had been anticipated. 'Both the MPAA and Warner Brothers report a total absence so far of the expected crank letters, [and] silence from the usual pressure groups', *Variety* reported on 13 July 1966.

Within a week of that report, seven hundred viewers at the Crescent Theater in Nashville had their enjoyment interrupted when police sergeant Fred Cobb (also a Baptist deacon) confiscated a reel of the film and mounted the cinema stage to explain that it was being banned for profanity: 'I represent the thinking of the good people of this town,' he told the Associated Press. Such incidents, however, proved to be the exception rather than the rule. The mainstream acceptance of the film was demonstrated the following year when it received eight Academy Award nominations, with Elizabeth Taylor being named Best Actress and Sandy Dennis Best Supporting Actress. (In Britain it did even better, winning the BAFTA Awards for Best Film, Best Actor and Best Actress.) The unexpected liberalism of the general public with respect to the film was further underlined in February 1973 when the CBS network gave it its television premiere – programming it at 9.00 pm Eastern time, directly after an episode of that somewhat more 'wholesome' family drama, *The Waltons*. Although some Southern network links refused to carry the film, reaction elsewhere was positive: the *New York Post* estimated that a staggering 39 per cent of that city's television audience had tuned in to watch, and reported that the local CBS station had received fewer than a hundred telephone calls of complaint (this despite the retention of the phrase 'hump the hostess'; although all the 'Jesuses' and most of the 'goddamns' were deleted from the soundtrack). 'Could it be that the TV audience is growing up?' asked the *Post's* Bob Williams, apparently oblivious to the fact that he was patronising his own readership (Williams 1973). The following year, in Britain, BBC Radio pushed the broadcasting envelope still further with an entirely uncut version of the play. This excellent production (discussed in detail in chapter 3) starred one of the original Broadway Marthas, Elaine Stritch. Also featured were two veterans of the 1964 London production, Ray McAnally (who had replaced Arthur Hill as George) and Pinkie Johnstone (Honey).

BROADWAY REVIVAL, 1976

In the theatre, the various manifestations of the original Barr–Schneider–Ritman franchise had finally exhausted their earning potential by 1965, and Barr thereafter began judiciously issuing licenses to regional producers. That year, for example, new versions appeared in locations as diverse as Los Angeles, Harrisburg and Winnipeg. New productions continued to pop up regularly at theatres across America throughout the later 1960s and early 1970s, in both commercial and 'not-for-profit' contexts. Indeed, *Virginia Woolf* became a staple choice for the new generation of subsidised regional theatres emerging at this time, since it served both of their twin financial imperatives: as a work of accepted artistic substance it helped to justify grants, while its almost cast-iron entertainment values kept core, subscription-paying audiences happy. In 1974, the play confirmed this new status when it was produced to acclaim at one of the first and most reputable of the not-for-profit theatres, Arena Stage in Washington, DC. Perhaps the most successful regional production of this period, though, was in Chicago in 1970, at the Ivanhoe Theatre, a small off-Loop venue (equivalent to off-Broadway) which was then only four years old. Critics declared George Keathley's revival superior both to the touring version of Schneider's production which they had seen in 1964, and to Mike Nichols' film. Suspicions of Midwestern prejudice against New York and Hollywood can be discounted when one notes that *Chicago Today* critic Roger Dettmer also declared that the Ivanhoe had with *Virginia Woolf* 'achieved a level of production and ensemble performance unparalleled in Chicago theater since 1953 – the duration of my own local memory span'. That word 'ensemble' – as opposed to 'virtuoso performance' or 'star turn' – is repeated insistently in reviews of Keathley's production, and seems to provide the clue to its startling success. Among the players was Ben Piazza, who had been the original title character in Albee's *The American Dream*, and was now revisiting the role of Nick which he had inherited from George Grizzard on Broadway in 1963.

The ubiquity and increasing familiarity of *Who's Afraid of Virginia Woolf?*, combined with the liberalisation of American culture during the 1960s, meant that the shock value which had initially helped the play to attract attention had quickly become far less pronounced. From Albee's point of view, this was no bad thing, allowing subsequent productions a greater opportunity to explore the play's subtler nuances and ambiguities. Most of the major revivals, from the 1970s to the 1990s, have sought in one way or another to bring out previously neglected aspects of the text, a revisionism which began in earnest in 1976 with the first (and to date only) Broadway revival, directed by Albee himself. The initial impetus for this production came from actress Colleen Dewhurst – arguably the greatest post-war interpreter of Eugene O'Neill's female characters – who had been offered a place as one of the matinee Marthas in 1962, but had been unavailable at the time. She had gone on to star in Albee's Broadway adaptation of Carson McCullers' *The Ballad of the Sad Cafe* in 1964, and in his *All Over* (1971), establishing herself as one of the author's favourite actresses. Dewhurst first essayed the part of Martha in 1965, in one of the first stock productions of *Virginia Woolf*, in Paramus, New Jersey, but she was sufficiently dissatisfied with her performance in that fairly low-profile outing to want to return to the part for a second attempt. She and her producer friend Ken Marsolais hit on the idea of asking Albee himself to direct, believing that this way 'we could create more excitement than might otherwise surround a revival' (Dewhurst 1997: 243). Albee seized on this proposal as an opportunity to mount a reconsideration of his play: 'it is only now, after twelve years', he reportedly told the actors on their first day of rehearsal, 'that I think I finally understand what I wrote' (Dewhurst 1997: 244).

Albee's 1976 production was significantly different from the original in a number of respects. For one thing, the play's renown now meant that the unusual production strategies employed by Barr and Wilder in 1962 were no longer necessary (Barr co-produced this time with Marsolais). The Broadway preview approach was replaced by the more conventional practice of out-of-town try-outs in New Haven and Boston, during which the cast worked their way into their roles, prior to the Broadway opening at the Music Box Theatre. On this occasion there were no censorship problems in Boston, even given that the author had now restored to the script his original, fairly liberal use of the 'f' word. Phrases such as 'frigging' and 'you mother' were suitably amended, with not one major critic making mention of the changes. (Asked why the printed version of the play has not by now been similarly 'restored', Albee simply shrugs that publishers are awkward about making such minor changes.) Beyond achieving this small victory for artistic freedom, though, Albee's decision to revisit the play as director also said a lot about his own development as an artist. In the previous year, he had made his first high-profile attempt it directing his own work, with the Broadway premiere of *Seascape*: 't didn't do too badly', he notes with characteristic understatement, t won the Pulitzer Prize' (Drake 1989: 4). Turning back to *Virginia Woolf* was an obvious way of building on this success, but was also e culmination of a self-education process that dated all the way back to the time of the original production. Although he has always stated publicly that he was very happy with what Schneider and his cast did with the play, it is also clear that he felt they had missed or underplayed certain important elements latent in the text. 'It occurred to me that an author who was a director as well could probably give a very accurate representation of the play he had in his head', Albee explained in a 1989 interview: 'So I staged a production of *The Zoo Story* in 1963 which, fortunately, played somewhere deep in Pennsylvania. I'd had no training. I just thought I could direct it. It was probably the worst production of any play of mine I'd ever seen' (Drake 1989: 4). Chastened, he began studying the methods used by other directors at work on his plays, a masterclass training which prepared him, by 1968, to attempt stagings of seven of his one-act pieces, for a university tour dubbed 'Albee Directs Albee'. By 1976 he felt confident enough to tackle his longest play.

Albee's objective in directing this revival was, in his own words, to 'clarify' certain things. He worked hard to ensure, for example, that *Virginia Woolf*'s humour was more readily apparent than it had been previously. In 1962, he felt, this aspect of the play had not been fully appreciated, partly because of its shock value at that time, but also partly 'because Alan Schneider was a very good director but he didn't

4. Ben Gazzara and Colleen Dewhurst in the 1976 production.

have much humour'. Having by now 'learned a fair amount from [Schneider] about directing, and about subtext primarily', Albee felt he was ready to explore his sense of the play's wit, and thus make up for what Schneider's version had lacked. He was also interested in exploring the sense of mutual passion and interdependence underlying George and Martha's surface antagonism: 'I felt that I would like people to have some sense of the sexuality of the relationship between the two of them, that there was a kind of physical warmth between them.' He found willing collaborators in Colleen Dewhurst and Ben Gazzara, who were old friends and used that bond fully in developing their characters' relationship. Both had also seen the original Broadway production, and wanted to provide a different interpretation. Dewhurst had greatly admired Hagen and Hill, but in Albee's opinion her drily self-possessed acting style 'made things more classical, a bit funnier' than in 1962 (Dewhurst 1997: 252). Gazzara was interested in a similar shift of tone because he had disliked the original production, feeling that its protagonists had created such

> an abrasive, hostile relationship [that] I didn't fully understand what was going on in the innards of those two characters. I told Edward about the things that disturbed me and he agreed. I asked, 'So why didn't you say something about it?' He said, 'I was so shy in those days, so young and so shy.' . . . Anyhow, Colleen and I worked on the love story, and I think it was successful. People who've seen the original, revivals, the movie, come backstage and tell me it's the first time they've ever felt the love between George and Martha. (*Buckley 1976*)

Critical reactions to this production indicate that Albee's intentions were made fully, triumphantly apparent to his audiences: 'much, much more so than in the original staging', wrote Clive Barnes in the *New York Times*, this version 'stresses the humor. It is now deliriously funny – perhaps the funniest play currently on Broadway.' The laughter, nevertheless, did not obscure the dominant impression that George and Martha 'are, when all is played out and washed up, a man and woman transparently, and even, in a burnt-out way, passionately in love with each other' (Barnes 1976).

Despite such praise, however, the production failed to ignite the hoped-for degree of interest at the box-office. This came as something of a surprise to the producers, since this was the first opportunity New York audiences had had to see *Virginia Woolf* in English since 1964. A touring Yugoslav company, Atelje 212, had presented it in Serbo-Croat at Lincoln Center in 1968, and in 1972 the locally based Spanish Theatre Repertory Company had inaugurated their work at Gramercy Arts Theatre with a critically acclaimed production of *¿Quién le teme a Virginia Woolf?*, but understandably enough these had not attracted large general audiences. The year 1976 had seemed like an opportune moment for a Broadway revival, but the Music Box run survived for only four months. 'In July of 1976, the bicentennial year, we closed', Colleen Dewhurst remarks in her autobiography: 'Perhaps the nation was too eager for some sort of celebration – even a false one – to embrace so much of the ugliness and beauty of the human condition.' She also concluded that she and Ken Marsolais had 'misjudged the power of the film which had been perfectly done nine years previously . . . By now, the material had become too familiar. Perhaps twelve years indeed wasn't a long enough time to bring in a revival, even with Edward directing' (Dewhurst 1997: 248).

LOS ANGELES, 1989

The spectre of the film version has continued to haunt subsequent stage productions, with critics regularly comparing stage performances to the one embalmed on screen. Moreover, given the experience of 1976 and the intense financial pressures of Broadway production, there have (at time of writing) been no commercial New York revivals since that date. Instead, during the 1980s and 1990s, the most significant productions took place in London. The institutional and economic structures of the British theatre are such that subsidised, not-for-profit theatres are able to attract 'name' actors to play in classic revivals far more regularly than are their American counterparts. In London, the intention with such revivals is often to transfer the production to a commercial, West End theatre if the initial 'art house' run proves successful. Given the greater financial pressures on American theatres, however, there has been only one high-profile new stage version on US soil since 1976 (although low-profile not-for-profit productions have continued to appear periodically at regional theatres). In 1989, the Doolittle Theatre of Los Angeles presented a star cast headed by John Lithgow and Glenda Jackson.

Albee again chose to direct this production, and for particular reasons. Perhaps stung by the continuing complaints, from a minority of the critics of the 1976 revival, that the exorcism of the imaginary child was not dramatically plausible, he set about attempting to demonstrate, with fresh clarity, the centrality and relevance of 'the bit about the kid'. According to Colleen Dewhurst, it was the third act climax, relating to the child, about which Albee had been most specific in his direction on that occasion: 'he knew exactly what he wanted and exactly how he wanted it done' (Dewhurst 1997: 245). Yet as Albee explained to the *Los Angeles Times* while rehearsing the new production, his main concern in 1976 had been with uncovering the play's humour, whereas 'one of the things I'm making terribly clear in this production . . . is that these people are indeed bright enough, inventive enough and mutually supportive enough to be able to levitate a metaphor, if you will, of 21 years. That's terribly important. The play is about the death of that metaphor' (Drake 1989: 40). One could, perhaps, surmise that the firmness of Albee's insistence on this issue – one which, by 1989, precious few critics would have wished to contest anyway – betrays a certain insecurity about the play's construction on its author's part. He knows better than anyone that his creation of the child came fairly late in the process of writing, and that its death was not, therefore, what the play was 'about' initially.

Whether or not there is any truth in this supposition, the 1989 production was a disappointment for all concerned. It failed to prove Albee's point for him, and he lays the blame for this squarely at the feet of his leading lady: 'John Lithgow was wonderful, but Glenda Jackson retreated back to that thing that she can do very well, that ice cold performance. I don't know whether she got scared, but in rehearsal she was being Martha, and the closer we got to opening the less Martha she was.' Audiences and critics alike found the resulting tone of the production coldly off-putting: 'No actors have ever done the George and Martha show with more style', wrote *LA Times* critic Dan Sullivan (who, as a *New York Times* critic in the 1960s and 1970s, was in a position to know), 'but when it comes to making us care about George and Martha, a lot of people have done better. Jackson's enormous self-sufficiency as an actress keeps us from feeling that there's anything under Martha's scorn but more scorn – she may be hurting, but she's in perfect control of herself' (Sullivan 1989: 10). Albee went straight on to re-direct this production in Houston, Texas, using an entirely new cast, all of whom had understudied at the Doolittle. Understandably, though, the project had lost something of its momentum. As Sullivan put it, audiences went to the Los Angeles *Virginia Woolf* 'expecting a 7 or 8 on the Richter scale', but found that it yielded 'only a 3 or 4'.

NATIONAL THEATRE, LONDON, 1981

Actor problems also dogged the two major British revivals of *Virginia Woolf* in the 1980s, productions which again attempted to present the play with a fresh perspective. The first of these was presented in 1981 by the National Theatre, whose decision to programme the play was based in large part on the realisation that it had not been seen in London, professionally at least, in a generation. Joan Plowright, cast as Martha, summed up the prevailing feeling in the show's programme notes: 'It needs doing again. My own children have never had the chance to see it.' The selection of Nancy Meckler to direct, however, was indicative of a generational shift of a different sort. As the first woman ever to direct a mainstage production at the National, she was conscious that a certain symbolic weight had been attached to her, and while she had no intention of grafting any artificially feminist reading on to a play written several years before the emergence of a coherent women's rights movement, Meckler nonetheless felt the time was right for a reconsideration of *Virginia Woolf*'s central relationship. Albee himself provided her with the ammunition she needed. 'I met him in New York before I started rehearsing', she explains,

> and he said he'd never been happy with the original production, because he felt that Martha had been a harridan and a joke, and that George had been hen-pecked and a victim, and he thought that was wrong: he'd always wanted the contenders to be equally weighted. So I took that very seriously, and I tried to work against this whole idea that it's a play about this castrating female. I thought of it more in terms of the fact that she's very disappointed in him, in what she wants him to be, because as a woman of that period she doesn't perceive herself as someone who could accomplish anything. She's barren in the sense that she doesn't see herself as someone who could make a place for herself in the world.

Unfortunately, Meckler's admirable attempts to re-read Martha in a more sympathetic light, and to balance up her battles with George, were sabotaged somewhat by events beyond her control. Joan Plowright seemed like ideal casting as Martha, and Albee, who flew over in June to see try-outs of the production at Bath's Theatre Royal, still ranks her as the one British actress to do full justice to what he sees as a very 'American' role. It was, he says, 'a fine production. She was tough and vulnerable, and Paul Eddington was a good foil for her. It was a nice company.' Plowright, however, backed out of the production on 10 July, the very day it was due to open at the National's Lyttelton Theatre in London, citing a throat infection. On 22 July, the National announced a new opening date for late August, to give her time to recover. Plowright responded within twenty-four hours with an announcement that – having consulted specialists – she had pulled out for good, in order to avoid any recurrence of her overstrained

5. Paul Eddington as George in the 1981 National Theatre production, London.

vocal condition. 'I never knew if that was the reality of the situation', Meckler notes, 'because she kind of implied to me that there was a story there that she'd never had a chance to tell me.' Albee, however, is in no doubt that the problem was not Plowright's throat but her husband, Lord Olivier. 'Himself', Albee reports, came to see one of the Bath previews:

> The next day, Joan asked awkwardly – we had breakfast together – she said, 'it's this simple, Edward. Joan Plowright can go to London with this role. Lady Olivier can't.' The rumour was that he had threatened to leave her if she did it. And I said 'well, gee, that's all right, because I hired Joan Plowright'. And she said, 'unfortunately you ended up with Lady Olivier'. And so she pulled out.

Meckler queries this version of events, pointing out that Plowright did perform previews in London, one of which Olivier also attended: 'I met him in the lounge and we chatted. He said he wasn't sure she had the third act yet. He was very professional, you know? But at that time he was so ill, there were certain days when he was quite reasonable and other days when he wasn't.' There was also the problem, well known in British theatrical circles, of a certain tension between Olivier, who had been instrumental in founding the National Theatre, and its then artistic director, Peter Hall. If Plowright did pull out for fear of upsetting her sick husband (and this remains speculative), it was a sadly ironic end to a promising performance built on the search for a marital battle that was 'equal'.

The National Theatre production reopened as scheduled on 27 August 1981, with Margaret Tyzack in the role of Martha. Tyzack, then best known for her work in Stratford, Ontario, had been recommended by Paul Eddington, who knew her well, and she was rehearsed quickly into the part. Meckler is very complimentary about her performance, as were many of the critics, but it is clear that director and actor did not see eye to eye over the production's objectives. Though Meckler felt 'a major, major commitment' to ensuring that Martha be seen in a more understanding light, Tyzack went on record in the *Guardian* with her insistence that 'I prefer gut reaction to arty-farty talk [about] the sterility of America in the 1960s and the position of women at that time' (Tyzack 1981). That reliance on 'gut reaction' also meant that Tyzack displayed little of the considered subtlety which – by all accounts – had marked Plowright's approach. Despite Meckler's best intentions, Paul Eddington's George became the undisputed star of the show, with a performance which was both sympathetic and immensely entertaining, handling the wit of Albee's dialogue with the kind of timing and emphasis one would expect from one of England's finest comic actors. A production which had begun as an attempt to reconsider Martha thus wound up as a showcase for one of the great readings of George.

YOUNG VIC, LONDON, 1987

The Young Vic's 1987 production also resulted in the stage being dominated by George, this time played by Patrick Stewart, at the expense of Billie Whitelaw's Martha. It was an experience which not only unbalanced the play but engendered long-lasting bitterness among the participants. Whitelaw, who had carved a formidable reputation for herself as the foremost interpreter of Samuel Beckett's monologue plays, but as a result had not performed opposite another stage actor for several years, had been approached by the Young Vic's director, David Thacker, about making a return to full-fledged 'play' acting. They selected *Virginia Woolf*, and together settled on Stewart, a respected Shakespearean actor, when Ronald Pickup proved to be unavailable for the role of George. From the start of rehearsals, however, Whitelaw felt isolated, believing that Thacker's main directorial 'twist' on the play – his insistence on having it performed in-the-round – was misguided. 'I felt this would make it far more difficult for all of us to create the play's *trapped* feeling', Whitelaw explains in her autobiography: 'I tried to persuade David to do it with an apron stage, or a thrust stage, but both he and Patrick were in no doubt: In-the-Round was the right way. For me, that may have been the beginning of feeling at odds and out-of-synch with both leading man and director' (Whitelaw 1995: 169). Whether or not Whitelaw was correct about the staging (an approach discussed in chapter 3), the men's failure to take her feelings into account seems to have been a serious misjudgement. The lack of communication escalated as rehearsals progressed, and Whitelaw became increasingly bewildered by Thacker and Stewart's insistence on discussing in minute detail interpretive questions which 'seemed to me as plain as a bloody pikestaff' (Whitelaw 1995: 170). Unable to get a grip on the production or her part, and feeling that Thacker was offering her no assistance, she became isolated and extremely anxious, so much so that – just days before the show opened – she took the extraordinary step of confessing to the press that she was

at the point where I'm saying to myself I'm never going to act again . . .
I'm sorry but I've never been in a state like this and there's nothing I can
do about it. I'm losing weight, I can't sleep, I can't watch telly and I
haven't read the papers in weeks . . . I can hear in my head what it should
be, but when it doesn't come out of my mouth as I hear it and my body
doesn't move as I want, it just drives you mad. (*Whitelaw 1987*)

The production was not quite the disaster such anxiety might
suggest, and opened as scheduled to fairly good reviews, with Patrick
Stewart and Thacker's in-the-round staging drawing most of the
praise. However, talk of a West End transfer after the limited season
four-week Young Vic run was quickly abandoned: Stewart recalls that
this was because Whitelaw did not wish to continue with the part any
longer than she had to; Whitelaw, conversely, recalls Stewart preparing for a rapid departure for Los Angeles, having been offered the
lucrative lead role in the new television series, *Star Trek: The Next
Generation*. Both claim the other's decision to quit informed their
own wish not to continue with the production; Stewart even implies
that, in better conditions, he might have been tempted to turn down
Star Trek. Whatever the truth, though, the experience has continued
to haunt both actors ever since. Whitelaw's confidence in her theatrical abilities was shattered, particularly by a crippling case of stage
fright which developed in the second week of the run (she began to
blank her lines at the same point every night, and had to rely on
Stewart to cover for her). 'I began to feel there was no longer a place
for me in the theatre at all', she wrote in 1995: 'since then, except for
my one-woman Beckett evenings, I've never set foot on a stage again'
(Whitelaw 1995: 172). In a 1997 interview, Stewart also recalled the
play as 'a bitter and sad subject [that] I cannot get out of my mind',
but primarily because it felt like unfinished business:

I simply connected with that role. It became for me among the three or
four most important theatrical experiences of my career – actually, I
would say one or two . . . I'd only played it for four weeks, and throughout the seven years I was doing [*Star Trek*], I fantasized about doing the

play again. When the production in Los Angeles was mounted with Glenda Jackson and John Lithgow, it was so painful to me that I couldn't bring myself to drive down the street past the theatre where it was playing . . . It is a very, very great play . . . and there's not a day goes by when I don't think about it. (*Zinman 1998: 68*)

ALMEIDA THEATRE, LONDON, 1996

Albee himself did not see the Young Vic production, but was angry over the distress it caused to Whitelaw, and at its failure to move to a longer run, since he believes that it takes several weeks of playing for a performance of *Virginia Woolf* to find the right groove and realise its full potential. Consequently, when the Almeida, another small, London-based art theatre, requested permission to mount a new production in 1996, he stipulated that he would only agree if a West End transfer was guaranteed. With Albee back in fashion following the international success of his 1994 Pulitzer Prize-winner *Three Tall Women*, he was in a strong position to make such demands, and a four-month run at the Aldwych Theatre was scheduled to follow the month at the Almeida. The resulting production added further momentum to the Albee renaissance, attracting rave reviews by striking that elusive balance between star-studded cast and genuinely co-operative, ensemble-oriented playing.

The Almeida production was initially suggested by a member of the theatre's board, Dame Diana Rigg, the former TV Avenger who was herself enjoying a renaissance in fortunes following recent lead performances in London productions of *Medea* and *Mother Courage*. The Almeida, which has a policy of programming star actors in plays they have special interest in, took little persuading that this would be Rigg's next great moment. However, the attendant danger of the show becoming an imbalanced star vehicle was counteracted by two other personnel decisions: the casting of David Suchet, another highly respected actor best known for his television work (as the title character in the Agatha Christie spin-off *Poirot*), and the choice of Howard Davies as director. Davies, whose work with the National Theatre, in particular, has made him one of the most accomplished British directors of the last two decades, had been wanting to tackle *Virginia Woolf* for some time, but had been stymied by the apparent reluctance of the National's artistic director, Richard Eyre, to programme it. On hearing of the Almeida's plans, he wasted no time in persuading them to hire him. From the outset, Davies was very clear about creating a four-way ensemble cast: 'I think the history of the play is that, because women don't get great roles generally, it's been used by a certain section of actresses who've gone "this is my play and everybody else can go hang". Well, that's not the way we did ours.'

Like Nancy Meckler before him, Davies had a distinctly political perspective in mind in his approach to the play. Part of a generation of British theatre professionals who had emerged during the 1970s, when the National was committed to producing the highly politicised playwriting of Edward Bond, Howard Brenton, David Edgar and others, Davies had raised many eyebrows when – in the 1980s – he began exploring the then unfashionable work of major American dramatists, most notably with his landmark 1988 Lyttelton revival of *Cat on a Hot Tin Roof*. For Davies, though, such choices were entirely consistent with his earlier interests. He describes *Cat*, for example, as 'a metaphor for American corruption and lying', and contests the critical tendency to depoliticise the work of writers like Williams and Albee: 'these people are so sharp, so bright, so politically aware that it inevitably informs their writing. With *Virginia Woolf* you know Edward has constructed this specific social critique.'

For Davies, then, the imperative in directing the Almeida production was to emphasise and draw out the myriad ways in which power – whether afforded through knowledge, seniority, youthful energy, sexuality or simply force of will – is manipulated by the play's various combatants. The performativity of Albee's language, the effects of his characters' 'speech acts', was arguably made clearer here than in any previous production. Indeed, the self-conscious theatricality of this version was foregrounded to such an extent that Rigg and Suchet took to bowing to each other during the curtain call, before acknowledging the applause of the audience. More significant, however, was Davies' attention to the strategic importance of Nick and Honey, and their function as the 'audience' for whose attention George and Martha compete in their verbal battle for domination. If Nancy Meckler had sought to even out the balance between the leads, Davies took this egalitarianism a step further by emphasising the *four-way* dynamics of the piece, and succeeded in finding a very finely balanced interplay among all four members of his cast. Clare Holman, who added Honey to an already impressive list of credits (including Abigail Williams in *The Crucible* and Harper in *Angels in America*, both at the National Theatre), stresses that the precision of this production was in large part a result of a very democratic, co-operative spirit which Davies succeeded in fostering in rehearsal:

> I suppose Diana and David could have decided to treat [Lloyd Owen and me] as secondary, but I think because of Howard's direction, and because they somehow knew that's what the play demanded, they were incredibly generous. You know it's a bit like a dance, that play: if somebody wants to move, then another person will stand up and say, 'well if you move there then that means I have to change that.' And nobody was scared to do that, nobody was scared to stand up and say, 'hang on'. There was a negotiation that went on, via Howard, and I really think that helped the production. Its success was very much to do with the ensemble.

Albee was periodically in attendance at rehearsals for the Almeida production, and declared in the programme note that it was 'among the very finest of the hundred or so productions of the play which I have seen' (Albee 1996). Most of the critics concurred, heaping praise on the entire cast, and the public was similarly responsive. When one considers the various imbalances of the other productions discussed in this chapter, it seems that – with the possible exception of Albee's own 1976 revival, of which there is unfortunately no permanent recording – the Almeida version was arguably the most complete and fully realised to date. The production was so highly regarded that a Broadway transfer was also seriously mooted, but these plans were shelved owing to Rigg's disinterest and Albee's understandable scepticism about having an all-British cast play such all-American roles in New York. At the time of writing, though, Howard Davies – who directed the world premiere of Albee's *The Play About the Baby* at the Almeida in the summer of 1998 – remains the first-choice candidate to direct an American cast in a projected Broadway revival of *Virginia Woolf*. Albee's current producer, Elizabeth Ireland McCann, is in no doubt that if such a production happens, it will be a very important one, if only because 'this might be the last major revival of *Virginia Woolf* in Edward's lifetime'.

NOTES

1 Letter from Donald Albery to Richard Barr, dated 30 April 1963. Richard Barr papers, Billy Rose Theatre Collection, Lincoln Center. Subsequent citations from the correspondence over London censorship are all from the papers in this collection.
2 Undated memo from Albery to Barr.
3 Letter from Barr's office to Albery, dated 3 November 1963.
4 Initial, undated, memo from Lord Chamberlain's office to Albery.
5 Albee cited in a letter from Anne Jenkins, general manager of Piccadilly Theatre, to the Lord Chamberlain's office, 3 February 1964.
6 Letter from Albery to Barr, 5 February 1964.

CHAPTER TWO

'WALPURGISNACHT'
THE CAULDRON OF CRITICISM

Having looked at the nuts-and-bolts details surrounding *Virginia Woolf*'s major productions in the US and UK, I intend in this second chapter to elucidate some of the debates generated by those productions, particularly among newspaper reviewers and cultural commentators. The goal is to provide a kind of critical biography of the play, mapping some of the ways in which understandings of it have shifted over time, as new productions have provided fresh opportunities for revision of opinion. Although some might argue that such an analysis of critical responses is extraneous to an account of a play's actual production history, it seems to me – conversely – that the performance of a play cannot be separated from the conditions of its interpretation. As reader-response theorist Stanley Fish has argued, a work of art only acquires significance and cultural currency through its reception by a variety of different 'interpretive communities' (see Bennett 1990: 42–3).

In the theatre that concept has particular relevance, because different 'communities' of interpreters are mingled bodily in the auditorium and become immediately aware of each other's responses. In the case of the opening night of the original Broadway production of *Virginia Woolf*, for example, the press critics must have been acutely aware that their usual authority as the arbiters of taste and quality had been significantly undermined by the ten preview nights. Those performances, attended primarily by the distinct 'communities' of invited theatre people and lower-income bargain-hunters, had resulted in considerable pre-opening excitement about the show. Some of the critics seem to have been caught up in that mood, while others – as we shall see – were clearly repulsed by it. None of them,

78

however, gave the play itself an unqualified seal of approval. In hindsight, it is clear that the status of Albee's play as a modern classic was established less by the critical acclaim it received on its first appearance than by its success at the box-office. Public enthusiasm for this avowedly 'difficult' play obliged an initially ambivalent critical fraternity to come round – over a period of years or even decades – to a level of endorsement of the play which it was at first loath to grant. This is a two-way process, though, and critical responses have also, inevitably, been very significant in shaping public interest, both by informing understandings of the play's 'meaning' and by stirring controversy. 'I am cynic enough to realize that when I elaborate on the depravity and obscenity of this play . . . I am helping the box office', wrote one tabloid reviewer in 1962: 'Okay – let it boom!' (Chapman 1962b). Similarly, in the longer term, the debates initiated by early critics have gone on to shape the terms of reference by which subsequent discussions have been conducted. Later commentators have necessarily been obliged to engage with those terms, and thus to some extent reinscribe them, even when seeking to propose alternative perspectives.

A further point to stress at the outset of this chapter is that, while audiences always play a fundamental role in shaping the perceived meaning and significance of any production, this play is one which places audiences in an unusually 'active' position as witnesses to the events occurring onstage. As Michael Smith astutely observed in his *Village Voice* review of the premiere production, '*Who's Afraid of Virginia Woolf?* is, subtly but critically, a new kind of play', in that it presents an apparently naturalistic scenario while deviating significantly from naturalistic convention: 'Albee has thrown out the fundamentally sentimental means – basically, making the audience identify with the hero or heroine – by which the ordinary naturalistic play "moves" its audience' (Smith 1962: 17). The patent unpleasantness of all four of Albee's characters makes such simple identification distinctly problematic. Yet if audience members cannot easily locate a figure on to which to project their sympathies, they necessarily become more aware of their own position as viewers, or even voyeurs. Indeed, for Michael Smith it was clear that the spectators themselves became an integral part of the event enacted: 'We are not moved or entertained by the play, we are transfixed . . . We are drawn smoothly into a world that we manage only to skirt in our ordinary lives, and then the gates are locked behind us.'

Smith's review was by far the most sophisticated and insightful of the early responses to *Virginia Woolf* (as one might expect from a commentator who became one of the most articulate defenders of New York's experimental theatre during the 1960s, and who in 1964 wrote the review that 'discovered' Sam Shepard). Yet his analysis was borne out by the comments of some more traditionalist critics, whose uncomfortable guilt at having been drawn in by the play's unorthodox pleasures manifested itself in accusations that Albee was somehow hypnotising his audiences into some kind of malign thralldom. 'Hateful is the proper word for *Whose Afraid of Virginia Woolf?*' wrote *Guardian* critic Philip Hope-Wallace after watching the 1964 British premiere: 'Hateful and shamefully funny and hideously watchable.' Such fulminations make it clear that the *performative effects* of George and Martha's word games are felt not only by Nick and Honey but by those witnesses sitting beyond the proscenium. With the earliest productions in particular, audiences found themselves confronted, to what was then an unprecedented degree, by vitriolic abuse and emotional manipulation being enacted for their entertainment (these events would not be taking place were they not paying money to bear mute witness to them). Since this linguistic aggression served no clear, thematic 'point' by which one could comfortably rationalise it and set it at a distance, it instead appeared to many to be gratuitously self-demonstrative. With the spectator having no obvious right of response to being implicated, without consent, into this spectacle of abuse (besides walking out of the theatre, and thus running the risk of performatively branding oneself a prude), many responded with shock and disgust, even while acknowledging the theatrical force of the play.

Critics seeking the moral high ground in the early 1960s sought to defuse their unease not only by scapegoating the play's then-unusual degree of profanity, but by concocting various speculative subtexts for the play so as to explain and contain its impact. These, as we shall see, included accusations of obscenity, fakery, decadence, and disguised homosexuality. In reflecting a general unwillingness to acknowledge that 'real' married couples might actually behave this way, these reactions pay testament to the impact of the play in cutting through the hypocritical social niceties of the post-Eisenhower years: Albee had succeeded in hitting a cultural nerve with devastating (if unwitting) accuracy. With the benefit of hindsight, the early critical disputes over *Virginia Woolf* read like early salvos fired in a culture war which would escalate rapidly during the 1960s, to the point where Albee himself looked more like an old-guard liberal than the dangerous and irresponsible young turk many initially took him to be. Subsequent productions occasioned gradual revisions of the more hostile critical positions, and by the 1970s, with American culture at large transformed by the events of the intervening years, *Virginia Woolf* no longer seemed nearly so shocking. As a result, though, audiences were more able to see past the surface pyrotechnics to the poignancy and broken-backed love underlying George's and Martha's dysfunctionality. By that stage it was also clear – with a good half-dozen more Albee plays in the public arena, none of which boast anything like the profanity of *Virginia Woolf* – that his characters' use of foul-mouthed vitriol was not simply a gratuitous stylistic indulgence but was integral to the peculiar impact of the play.

REALLY ABSURD OR ABSURDLY REAL?

It is perhaps difficult to appreciate, in the light of its historically proven success, just how unorthodox a play *Who's Afraid of Virginia Woolf?* would have seemed on Broadway in 1962: the critical responses of all hues are worthy of examination if only for the light they shed on what was considered 'normal' for mainstream theatre in that period. Albee's play was troubling not only because of his characters' uninhibited behaviour, but because it blurred and destabilised the familiar categorical boundaries between Broadway's staple diet of domestic naturalism and the overt experimentalism of the new avant garde. Albee himself, following the success of his early one-act plays, was assumed to be working in the latter camp, and indeed was seen as the chief American exponent of the latest European 'fad' – the theatre of the absurd. What then was he doing writing a play about university professors and their wives?

The term 'theatre of the absurd' had been coined by Martin Esslin as the title for his book of 1961, which grouped together the disparate work of Beckett, Ionesco, Adamov and others. The common concern of these dramatists, as Esslin saw it, was with dramatising the futility and comical absurdity of human existence in a chaotic, godless universe, and his book immediately provided ammunition to those American critics – liberal and conservative alike – who regarded these new works as a nihilistic and irresponsible avoidance of post-war realities, imported from a crumbling Europe. Several critics quickly made the connection between Esslin's critique and the work of off-Broadway playwrights including Albee, Jack Gelber and Arthur Kopit (Esslin included these three in a revised edition of his book in 1968), and this link only increased the suspicion with which they were regarded by many in the cultural mainstream. Albee's qualified embracing of the term in a *New York Times* article in February 1962 was thus knowingly provocative in more than one respect:

> I would submit that the Theatre of the Absurd, in the sense that it is truly the contemporary theatre, facing as it does man's condition as it is, is the Realistic theatre of our time; and that the supposedly Realistic theatre – the term used here to mean most of what is produced on Broadway – in the sense that it panders to the public need for self-congratulation and reassurance and presents a false picture of ourselves to ourselves, is, with an occasional very lovely exception, really and truly the Theatre of the Absurd. (*Albee 1962: 172*)

As if he had not offended enough, Albee went on to insist that the Broadway audience 'is so pre-conditioned by pap as to have cut off half its responses. . . . For it is a lazy public which produces a slothful and irresponsible theatre' (1962: 173). His credentials as an angry young iconoclast thus firmly established, Albee's arrival on Broadway with *Virginia Woolf* was inevitably going to be viewed widely as an invasion of the citadels, a slap in the face of the established Broadway culture. Nor did it help that the play had such a blatantly absurd (or simply 'smart-aleck') title. As both an intellectual witticism and a play on popular culture ('Who's Afraid of the Big Bad Wolf?'), the phrase had a performative frisson all its own when erected on a midtown theatre hoarding. Clinton Wilder, for one, was worried that Albee was prejudicing the play's reception simply by insisting on that title: playwright Doric Wilson, who was then working as an unpaid production assistant to Richard Barr, vividly recalls 'riding in a cab through the Village with Clinton not long before the show opened, and he was telling me that I had to tell Richard and Edward that they had to change the title. The title had to go!'

Albee himself has no recollection of being asked to make such a change, but did engage in a certain amount of pre-opening damage limitation by attempting to flatter the mainstream press critics with their own (questionable) magnanimity. In another article for the *New York Times*, written with the premiere fast approaching, he insisted that whether the play opened on or off Broadway should not matter, because 'all in all, things are fair' in New York: 'in a responsible press there is no double standard of judgment . . . a play is a play and must be so judged' (Weatherby 1962). Yet this somewhat disingenuous statement conveniently avoided the fact that Albee's ideas of what constituted 'a play' might well be very different from that of the press. Confronted with the trappings of a domestic drama, most of the critics instantly assumed that they understood the 'rules' by which *Virginia Woolf* operated, and judged it – without query or further consideration – according to the most banal standards of naturalism. To the *New York Mirror*'s Robert Coleman, for example, the play was simply a depiction of a party in which the hosts 'have such bad taste as to reveal their innermost secrets to their embarrassed guests . . . It turns out that the ineffectual history prof's spouse is a nympho and a dipso, who suffers from the delusion that she has a son who has been driven away by her husband's action.' Deprived of the familiar pleasure of sentimental identification with the protagonists, Coleman and many of his colleagues responded with bemusement as to why the depiction of these characters should be considered of anything other than prurient interest to an audience.

There was also an almost unseemly haste in several critics' need to point out that George and Martha's unhealthy relationship bore no similarities to any they had ever come across in 'real life', and that this fact rendered the play a mere sordid curiosity. (Presumably the same would not have been claimed of, say, Mr and Mrs Macbeth.) While doubting 'whether such characters actually exist', *Variety's* Hobe acknowledged that 'evidently young Albee believes they do, and presumably he is writing from personal observation'. The play, he thus decided, 'establishes Albee as a gifted playwright, if an unenviable individual.' In *Women's Wear Daily*, Thomas Dash offered a variation on the same theme by querying whether this really was 'a true depiction of life among the intellectuals who teach America's student body'. He concluded that even if it was (and if so, then heaven help 'the undergraduates and the uneducated of the lower depths'), 'then the play does not have too much universality or even too much relevance'. The general consensus from a whole section of the press was that, if Albee's protagonists were to be considered believable characters at all, then it was as freaks in urgent need of therapy: 'Martha and George are evidently masochists' (Dash); 'This is a sick play about sick people. They are neurotic, cruel and nasty. They really belong in a sanitarium for the mentally ill rather than on a stage' (Chapman 1962a).

Interestingly, the critics of the play's London opening, sixteen months later, were generally more willing to accept that such characters might exist. The anonymous drama critic of *The Times* even went so far as to suggest that 'anyone with experience of marital warfare will take grim pleasure from Mr. Albee's mastery of its most advanced tactics'. It is difficult to say, however, whether such differences in attitude were thanks more to English frankness or to the advantage of knowing how successful the play had already been in America. And even in London, almost nobody bothered to query the assumption that the play was *intended* as a representative portrayal, be it of university life, modern marriage or psychotics. Of all those reviewing the premieres on either side of the Atlantic, only Walter Kerr of the *New York Herald Tribune* made any clear attempt to relate the play to Albee's supposed status as a charter member of the theatre of the absurd. In his initial review, seizing on the moment in which George 'shoots' Martha, only for the gun to produce a coloured parasol, Kerr remarked that 'the hatred that fills up empty lives (for want of anything better to fill them) is real. It is also absurd' (1962a). In his Sunday perspective piece, he attempted to clarify this rather lame assertion, arguing that Albee 'has here brought something of the Absurd's shrill surrender to unreason into the environment of the apparently reasonable . . . In the contrast between a plausible, even homey surface and the uninhibited spewing forth of its grossest underpinnings, the crack of comedy is heard' (1962b).

Even Kerr, however, seemed unable to extend this insight far: the 'absurd' was apparent to him in overtly theatrical moments such as that with the parasol, but could not be seen as something which might have affected (or infected) Albee's construction of the play as a whole. Like most of his colleagues, Kerr assumed that since *Virginia Woolf* appeared naturalistic, it should also be expected to conform to naturalism's familiar dramaturgical conventions, and was therefore flawed insofar as it did not. In a 1963 article examining responses to the opening production, Diana Trilling went so far as explicitly to insist that since 'nothing in the technique or in the stylistic manner of *Virginia Woolf* is anything *except* representational' (i.e. naturalistic), then it clearly needed to be judged according to the same rules as other 'representational' works, rather than on the 'metaphorical' level being used to interpret the work of, say, Harold Pinter (Trilling 1963: 81). The rules in question are all but listed in Kerr's exegesis of the play, the action of which – he insists – is all directed towards its third-act climax, where 'Mr. Albee attempts to synthesize his findings, to wrap them up coherently in a single telling image' which would sum up the play's content – its ruling themes of truth and illusion. And at this point, Kerr believes, 'we hear something false in the writing', since the revelation surrounding the imaginary child, 'the core of the phantasmagoria, the source of much broomstickery, is inadequate as a symbol: it has something of the sound of a feeble child's lie, feeble because he [Albee] does not believe he can get away with it' (1962b).

Kerr's analysis provides what is virtually a copybook summary of the sub-Ibsenite plot mechanics which in 1962 still dominated the Broadway 'straight play': the drama must clearly set out a conflict at the outset; it must build steadily toward a third act resolution of that conflict in which everything will be 'wrapped-up'; the wrapping-up must involve an 'adequate' restatement and summation of the play's content in the form of a ruling symbol; the wrapping-up must convince the audience with the inevitability of the cause-and-effect dramatic logic with which it is arrived at. Albee's failure to meet these requirements thus renders his play deeply flawed: 'It is a brilliant piece of writing', Kerr concludes, 'with a sizeable hole in its head' (1962a). His attitude is typical of that taken by most of the more positive early critiques of *Virginia Woolf.* The virtuoso dynamism of Albee's text, and the dazzling commitment with which Schneider's cast delivered it, were greatly to be praised, but the play as a whole was unwieldy and unforgivably lengthy, because so much of the word-play seemed entirely unnecessary either in elaborating exposition, forwarding plot or developing message. 'Probing, searing and absorbing as *Virginia Woolf* is, it could have been made even more taut by the compression of some of its excessive verbiage', thought Thomas Dash. The play's detractors were still more blunt: 'The main objections to it, as I see them', Roger Gellert argued in his *New Statesman* review of the London opening, 'are its inordinate length and its pretensions to surgical depth. In over three hours of playing time we cover about as much ground as an Angus Wilson short story.' Gellert's oddly mixed-metaphoric assumption that 'depth' must equate with 'ground covered' by the plot is a telling indicator of the largely unquestioned critical assumptions of the period.

Despite the fact that it is barely even mentioned in the first two acts, most reviewers concurred that the story surrounding George and Martha's imaginary child was – as the *New York Times*' Howard Taubman put it – the main 'pillar of the plot', and that as such it was 'too flimsy to support the climax'. For some reason, the 'trickery' involved in the revelation of the child's non-existence was a particular source of outrage for London critics, who felt that they had been led on to believe there was a great deal more to be discovered about the situation than is actually revealed. 'A great part of the excitement and tension of [Albee's] extraordinary play lies in the implicit suggestion that [George and Martha are] evil and criminal', wrote Harold Hobson in *The Sunday Times*, who had clearly expected skeletons to be de-closeted and murderous psychology to be revealed: 'It would have been infinitely more difficult to hold our attention fascinated and horrified (as he does) had he told us plainly at the beginning what he admits at the end: that they are mad.' The *Guardian*'s Philip Hope-Wallace added, 'damningly', that this ending 'provides not a drop of that resolution . . . which would atone for the long, degrading night of wrangling'.

Intriguingly, in his 1962 *Village Voice* review, Michael Smith had anticipated all these various objections to Albee's dramaturgy with pinpoint accuracy, while reminding his readers of Albee's credentials as an experimentalist. In a play 'about truth and illusion', Smith noted,

> the number one illusion is that this is a conventional play . . . It has a number of faults when it is seen as one, [but] these give the clue to what it really is . . . The first clue is the play's length. It goes on and on and on and on and on, with no real justification except completeness . . . The structure is something like variations on a theme, the theme being

> people destroying one another and the variations being four of the
> hilarious, vicious games that they play. The basic material is stated at the
> outset, and for the next three hours we go deeper into the familiar mire
> . . . After the first 45 minutes we are . . . practically numb, with no reli-
> able sense of time or of emotional balance. (*Smith 1962: 11, 17*)

Smith's assertion that the play is more 'a kind of ritual' than a conventional drama is notable for its foregrounding of the intensity of the
theatrical experience itself. The audience's loss of bearings, he suggests, mirrors the increasing intoxication and bewilderment of the
characters. Mainstream commentators, not surprisingly, did not leap
to concur with Smith's notion that the play left spectators feeling 'as if
. . . we were drugged or drunk', but his point about Albee being less
interested in linear dramaturgy than in a kind of musical circularity,
in theme and variation, gradually began to be picked up more widely.

John Gassner, for example, in reviewing the release of the 1963
CBS cast recording, offered the first sustained account of the
musical, rhythmic properties of the play's dialogue and structure.
The fact that *Virginia Woolf* is composed of 'a series of musico-dra-
matic movements', and that the lines are notable 'for their shape as
well as content and for their cadence as well as substance', becomes
more apparent in the recording than on stage, Gassner suggested,
'because the text comes at us naked, so to speak – that is, as pure
sound' (Gassner 1963: 40). By the time of the London opening in
1964, numerous reviewers were speaking rhapsodically of the play's
musicality in a way that the New York press had not even thought to:
'Mr. Albee is a musician. He has composed a long, 3½-hour quartet
for four voices in the key of marriage and he has done it with a beautiful and rare sense of form' (Lewis); 'each section of *Virginia Woolf*
is orchestrated with a most cunningly precise sense of dramatic
rhythm' (Nathan); '[the] language flows to the rhythm and discipline
of a Bach concerto' (Leonard); the action has 'the inexorability of a
Bruckner symphony' (P.H.). The analogies are wild stabs, and often
accompanied by objections to the play on more conventional
grounds, but – in the light of the play's undeniable success in New

York – the London critics were understandably keen to find ways of explaining its impact. The advantage of using music as a reference point, of course, was that the emotional drive of music depends entirely on structure, arrangement and performance. The task of discussing what *Virginia Woolf* might actually *mean* could thus be sidestepped by those critics who were becoming aware that conventional dramatic criticism – with its insistence on rationally explicable statement – could not readily account for Albee's achievement.

Yet if critics were gradually becoming aware that the play was distinguished primarily by its extraordinary and ambiguous use of stage dialogue, this realisation was of little help to Ernest Lehman in adapting *Virginia Woolf* to the screen. Lehman appears to have taken seriously the various critical objections to Albee's dramaturgical approach, since the film medium's emphasis on visually driven storytelling, as opposed to verbal complexity, meant that he had, necessarily, to find a way to emphasise the play's narrative line. Complaints about the play's length were, of course, instantly addressed by the fact that Lehman had to cut nearly an hour off the playing time simply to make it saleable as a movie. Thus, among numerous other excisions, he opted to trim large parts of the seemingly more aimless conversation in Act I, to shorten the climactic exorcism scene, and to remove an entire chunk of the latter part of Act II. All of these cuts operated to render the play somewhat more 'conventional' dramaturgically, since they operated to bring into clearer focus the material necessary to the linear progression of Albee's scenario. Many of the more traditionalist critics thus felt that the film's greater 'discipline' had improved on Albee's play. In her *Sunday Times* review, Dilys Powell commented that, where she had felt the stage version dragged on too long and too implausibly, 'the flow of the action' seemed clearer in the film. Powell saw such editing devices as the trip out to the roadhouse as improvements: 'personally I find these help the suspension of disbelief; not only does the pertinacity of the visitors become more plausible, the prison of character rather than scene becomes more inescapable' (Powell 1966).

On stage, of course, the 'prison of scene' is fundamental to the play's impact: like Nick and Honey, the audience themselves are incapable of escaping the claustrophobic intensity of this single-room encounter. They are also, crucially, unable to tell whether anything George and Martha tell them in this room is actually true, but in opening the play up for film, Lehman was faced with the question of whether or not Warner Brothers could afford to commit such disorientating ambiguities to film. It was feared that the general movie-going public would respond even more negatively than had many of the Broadway critics to a piece that lacked a 'proper' plot with an emotionally 'satisfying' resolution. Thus, in his early drafts of the screenplay, Lehman toyed with various flashback sequences, in an attempt to clarify the veracity of stories that remain ambiguous when told by Albee's characters. There was, for example, to have been a speakeasy scene in which George remembers seeing a young man ordering 'bergin' – a choice which would simultaneously have ruled out the possibility either that the story is pure fiction, or that George *himself* might have been the boy in question. Understanding that such changes would have seriously undermined the sense of mystery which is fundamental to the whole scenario, Mike Nichols ensured that such ideas were scrapped. He opted to shoot the entirety of George's bergin speech as a static medium close-up, a distancing effect which – far from clarifying the veracity of the story – placed the emphasis on Burton's *performance*, and obliged the audience (as in the theatre) to make up their own minds about its reliability.

Nichols also, still more importantly, intervened to prevent the imaginary child from becoming a real one. Lehman had literally written a closet into his screenplay, which did not contain a skeleton as such, but which was periodically to be indicated as 'significant' by George, Martha or the camera. During the exorcism scene, George would then fling the door open to reveal a bare space, which would be momentarily filled by a jump-cut flashback in which Martha sees a frail teenage boy hanging by the neck from the coat-rail. 'Jim is dead and you know it!' was to be George's clinching line. This was felt by some at Warner Brothers to be a less 'contrived' ending to the narrative than the one Albee had written. 'How lucky to get a chance to protect it', Nichols told an interviewer in reference to the imaginary child, 'from being turned into God knows what' (Leff 1981: 456).

The result of such interventions, however, was that the critics' objections to Nichols' film were again directed primarily at the source material, since it had been so 'faithfully' adapted. 'Whatever the shortcomings and annoyances in the film', Bosley Crowther concluded in the *New York Times*, 'they should be charged against the obscurities in Mr. Albee's work, rather than against the fairness of Ernest Lehman's script or the prescience of Mike Nichols's direction' (Crowther 1966). Ironically, even *Village Voice* critic Andrew Sarris came to the conclusion that Lehman had been too 'timidly faithful' in his adaptation, although on different grounds than those who had wanted the play made more conventionally palatable. With *Virginia Woolf* having become so commercially successful, its avant-garde *cachet* with the *Voice* had fallen, and Sarris all but dismissed the film as a sell-out on Albee's part: 'Why Jack Warner should be applauded for bringing a Broadway hit to the screen is beyond me.' In complete ignorance of the facts, Sarris snidely remarked that 'there was never any serious question of a major infidelity to Edward Albee's original text. Consequently many of the flaws in the film have been transcribed in all their intactness from the stage.' Interestingly though, the only such flaw Sarris can enumerate is that

> the third act of *Virginia Woolf* degenerates into hysterical charades which can be vulgarized by middle-brow audiences into conventional pieties. 'You couldn't have children of your own?' George Segal asks solicitously. 'Aha!' the audience responds. 'That's what all this yelling is about. They really love each other very much, but they can't have children. No, it's not just that. Their yelling is a form of communication. To show they're alive. That's what it all means.' (*Sarris, 1966*)

WHAT IT ALL MEANS

Sarris' remarks are cutting, but his implication that Hollywood might have doctored the script to make such sentimentalisation *less* likely seems laughable. Moreover, this particular mock-summary of 'what it all means' is actually rather sophisticated by comparison with most of the other propositions floating in the wake of the play's success. If the perceived inadequacies of *Virginia Woolf*'s premise and narrative mechanics were the main source of objection for some, for others it was the perceived triteness of the play's lessons for its audience. Still in thrall to the liberal message-play model pioneered by Ibsen, most critics assumed that Albee was trying to teach them something, to make a (constative) statement regarding a perceived 'truth', as opposed to exploring the (performative) dynamics involved in a messily human situation. The irony is that, since the play offers no clear message, many critics invented messages for it, and then came to the conclusion that they were being condescended to by Albee. 'The play's message is – or so I take it – that if we are to survive we must destroy all our illusions and make the best of reality, such as it is', Hugh Leonard wrote of the London opening in *Plays and Players*: 'But the play is too specific to embrace what Mr. Albee considers to be universal truths. Its aspirations are so enormous as to far out-range its author's intellectual powers.' Few reviewers stopped to ask whether it might be their own assumptions which were at fault, rather than Albee's competence.

One particularly telling aspect of this widespread dismissal of Albee's 'vision' was the uncomplimentary comparisons which numerous critics chose to make between *Virginia Woolf* and Eugene O'Neill's *Long Day's Journey Into Night*: the former's 'limited view of the human condition is obvious', wrote W. J. Weatherby, when contrasted with 'that other lengthy study of American society' (Weatherby 1962). Although Albee had had O'Neill's *The Iceman Cometh* in mind in writing the play, *Long Day's Journey* became the favoured reference point for a wide range of critics, thanks to the similarities in terms of length, family in-fighting, and claustrophobic living-room setting. First produced on Broadway only six years prior to *Virginia Woolf*, *Long Day's Journey* was still fairly fresh in the cultural memory, and its almost universal acceptance as the greatest-ever work of 'The Master' (as Weatherby calls him) made it a useful club with which to beat the 'pretensions' of Albee's play, which was deemed shallowly juvenile in comparison. Essayist Diana Trilling, for example, suggested that while both plays displayed a similar tone of bleak helplessness, there was a fundamental difference in 'truth' between them. 'Of the performance of O'Neill's drama which I witnessed I can say that I have never seen an audience at a modern play so profoundly shaken by the truth with which it had been confronted', Trilling wrote: 'No one is shaken by Mr. Albee's play. At most they are disquieted, which is a different order of emotion' (Trilling 1963: 86).

This curiously vague distinction is explained by Trilling's insistence that the relevance of the characters in *Virginia Woolf* was limited to the particularities of their social situation, whereas *Long Day's Journey Into Night* 'transcends the merely familiar or recognisable' to achieve 'momentous psychological and moral reality' (1963: 82). Trilling's choice of the phrase 'psychological reality' is key here – and indicative of yet more ingrained critical expectations. Besides *Virginia Woolf*'s other manifest sins (no 'proper' plot, no neatly summative dramatic symbol), this was a play in which character psychology and motivation remained uncertain, even at times opaque, rather than being explicated along rational lines of cause and effect. *Long Day's Journey*, of course, obeys this most familiar of naturalistic conventions: the whole play is geared toward the gradual revelation of how past traumas live on in the present. Yet the revelations about the pasts of George and Martha, Nick and Honey, are fragmentary and often unreliable. Albee's emphasis is on their behaviour in the ongoing present, and his inspiration for this approach was undoubtedly Beckett. When applied in an ostensibly naturalistic context, this removal of an analysable past flew in the face of the psychologism which had been wedded to the genre since its inception in the late nineteenth century. Hence Harold Clurman's objections in his *New Republic* critique that 'the characters have no life (or texture) apart from the immediate virulence of their confined action or speech . . . Vividly as each personage is drawn, they all nevertheless remain flat – caricatures rather than people' (Clurman 1962: 78). Clurman, a former director of the Group Theatre and champion of the Stanislavsky system, thus lambasts Albee for not joining the psychological dots like some Method acting exercise. One might reasonably respond (invoking Albee's own inversion of the terms 'realistic' and 'absurd') that it is absurdly unrealistic to expect the participants in a late-night drinking binge to reveal a coherent psychological narrative of their lives. Nevertheless, for both Clurman and Trilling, such 'failings' mean that, in the latter's words, 'Mr. Albee's characters did not speak a recognizable human truth' (Trilling 1963: 82).

Both of these influential commentators go on to conclude that Albee's message (since he must have one) is an *artificial* 'truth' rather than a genuinely *human* one; that his authorial statement is really only a reductive distillation of Martin Esslin's reductive distillation of Beckett, Ionesco *et al.* Marrying Albee's concern with illusion to Esslin's 'death of God' theme, Trilling comes up with a startling leap of interpretation completely unsupported by the play itself: 'what is wrong with self-deception for Mr. Albee is not that it robs us of the strength to struggle in our own best interests but that it provides life with a meaning it doesn't have. It gives life a content, and this, in Mr. Albee's view and in the view of most of the advanced writers of our time, is *a priori* a falsification; life has no content' (Trilling 1963: 85). Notwithstanding this, it seems that plays do have content and that is what this one's is: Trilling's objections to *Virginia Woolf* thus turn out to be less objections to anything Albee actually wrote than a priori objections to 'most of the advanced writers of our time' (or perhaps just Martin Esslin); this despite her denial of Albee's right to stand alongside those writers because his play is too straightforwardly naturalistic. Similarly, Harold Clurman accuses Albee of employing a 'slick and automatic' morbidity which borrows from avant-garde fashion without justifying itself: 'The right to pessimism has to be earned within the artistic terms one sets up; the pessimism and rage of *Who's Afraid of Virginia Woolf?* are immature. Immaturity coupled with a commanding deftness is dangerous' (Clurman 1962: 78).

A further twist here is that, despite the critical pronouncements on the characters' cartoonish lack of depth, the apparent need to invent neatly comprehensible meanings for *Virginia Woolf* resulted in a tendency among audiences to fill in the play's psychological details for themselves. The reviews of the 1966 movie version provide clear evidence that various more-or-less peculiar explanations for George and Martha's behaviour had evolved extra-textually in the period of popular debate following *Virginia Woolf*'s premiere. Several of the critics now seemed to take it as read that 'the crucial point in this drama is that the vulgar and snarling wife is a frightened, inhibited creature for all her brazen profanity' (Crowther 1966). The source of Martha's neuroses had been diagnosed along predictably pop-Freudian lines. 'The really relevant unseen character is not the son; it is Martha's father', insisted Stanley Kauffmann in the *New York Times*. 'It is he whom she idolizes and measures her husband against, it is his presence George has to contend with, in and out of bed. It is Daddy's power, symbolic in Martha, that keeps the visiting couple from leaving' (Kauffmann 1966c). Extending the same logic, Alvin Kernan decided that the imaginary child is Martha's phallus substitute, 'to use any way she wants' (Kernan 1967: 92). Its removal is thus a symbolic castration, which explains why George's exorcism traumatises her so. The absurdity of such assumptions was unwittingly pointed up in Edith Oliver's 1966 review of the film for *New York* magazine, which notes that, in the process of screen adaptation, 'Martha's incestuous feelings about her father have been either so pared down or so played down that one barely notices them.' It does not occur to her that such feelings might not actually have been apparent in the script to begin with.

The inverse of this phenomenon was that certain aspects of what Albee *had* written, and in particular his implicit critique of American social mores, was ignored or even denied in the play's reception. To British critic W. J. Weatherby it seemed evident from the play's Broadway premiere that this was 'a biting . . . view of American and perhaps of Western society', which, despite its other failings, was 'continually interesting as an uncompromising satire' (Weatherby 1962). Yet the American critics seemed universally oblivious to this dimension of the play, the continued marginalisation of which was made especially apparent by Ernest Lehman's screenplay adaptation, which opted to cut most of Albee's more explicit references to history and politics. Nor are such losses merely incidental to the trimming. For example, George's passing description of Honey's father's avarice as 'a pragmatic extension of the big dream' (88) is the single deletion from a long sequence of dialogue otherwise entirely free of cuts, and as such is clearly indicative of Lehman's careful removal of anything in Albee's text which openly queried ruling American myths. Since few had been willing to acknowledge these elements to begin with, though, it is hardly surprising that the effect of such deletions was lost on reviewers. 'As far as I could tell, little has been lost and a lot gained in the cutting' (Oliver 1966).

Conversely, but presumably for much the same reasons, foreign critics have proved all too willing to view *Virginia Woolf* as a scathing critique of American society, rather than as a play whose scenario might have broader implications. Indeed, when the play premiered in Poland in 1965, it proved acceptable to the communist authorities only because it was assumed that the characters' flailing viciousness was being presented as a social product of the West. 'There was a storm of objections to this "pathological" play as being one step removed from decadence', the *Christian Science Monitor* noted of the Gdansk premiere: 'Since the setting is America, however, this near-decadence can be played in Poland, and a Warsaw company has now also added Albee's play to its repertoire' (Pond 1965). This cultural denunciation factor resulted in a curious experience for New York

6. Liljana Krstic as Martha, Slobodan Perovic as George, Ruzica Sokic as Honey and Vlada Popovic as Nick in the Yugoslav production by Atelje 212 which toured to Lincoln Center in 1968. Note Peter Pasic's minimalistic, non-naturalistic set design, which foregrounds a bar (and thus the characters' consumption of alcohol).

audiences in 1968 when another Eastern bloc company, Yugoslavia's Atelje 212, presented its repertoire at Lincoln Center. Reviewers were initially somewhat taken aback at seeing *Virginia Woolf* played as a kind of grotesque parody of American culture. Against 'a three-piece living room set of matching green naugahyde', Nick was dressed in a 'nipped at the waist double-breasted business suit' and Honey in 'black velveteen mini with a pseudo-ermine wrap . . . remind[ing] you most inappropriately of Edie Adams's parody of Marilyn Monroe' (Sullivan 1968). On further reflection, the New York critics chose to put these rather distorted Americanisms down to the understandable misconceptions Europeans might have gleaned from Hollywood exports, and to emphasise that 'the play's interest must surely be international' (Watts 1968). There is no doubt, however, that many foreign critics have continued to view *Virginia Woolf* as a peculiarly American piece. 'We Britishers are insulated from the full power [of the play] by our different manners', the *Spectator* commented smugly of the National Theatre's 1981 revival (*LTR* 1981: 440). The *Daily Telegraph* concurred that 'the play stands as an indictment of the barrenness, the immorality and the greed in American society', while the *Guardian* suggested that this 'is a requiem for a country that simply cannot bear to look the truth in the face' (*LTR* 1981: 438–9). The prevalence of such comments in response to this production, in particular, suggests a peculiarly English mix of superiority and denial, given the context of the attempts that Prime Minister Margaret Thatcher was making in the early 1980s to bring British economic attitudes more in line with America's.

WHO'S AFRAID . . .?

In America, in the 1960s, *Who's Afraid of Virginia Woolf?* tended to be viewed less as a critique of the nation's decadence than as a symptom of it. Since the play, according to established critical standards, lacked either psychological or philosophical depth and was not therefore morally serious – since it was not actually 'a good play' – then its popularity with audiences had to be indicative of cultural decline. The tabloid reviewers wasted no time in pointing this out in 1962: the *New York Mirror*, for example, deplored the play as a 'sordid and cynical dip into depravity' which would appeal to spectators who 'enjoy watching the wings being torn from human flies', while noting with horror that 'the first night audience loved it. There were salvos of bravos' (Coleman). Such damning comments, however, were by no means limited to conservative pressmen: in a 1963 editorial article for the *Tulane Drama Review*, radical theatre advocate Richard Schechner savaged both the Broadway production and its audiences, with the declaration that 'Albee runs because we see in his work a reflection [of ourselves] which pleases us . . . We eagerly exaggerate our naughtiness into hard vices and our vices into perversities. Oh, if only we could play "humiliate the host" or "hump the hostess" as do the heroes of *Virginia Woolf,* if only our lives were truly *that* decadent!' (Schechner 1963: 7–8). Similarly, Diana Trilling reported that the 'decent respectable middle class people' attending the play seemed to crave association with its aura of sophistication: as a member of the intelligentsia, she reports, 'I was aware of a certain cozy sense of cultural superiority because I was "in" on Mr. Albee's idiom' (Trilling 1963: 87).

Such commentaries appear to have some degree of justification, at least as far as audience reaction was concerned. Dorothy Kilgallen's opening night review for the *New York Journal-American* established the snob agenda with alarming clarity by declaring that 'Edward Albee is going to cause more dinner table debates than Tennessee Williams ever inspired. . . . People who are reluctant to face life will be reluctant to face this play. But the true sophisticates and the intellectuals and the unafraid should keep its box office buzzing for many a moon.' When the production transferred to London, *The Spectator* suggested that the title *Who's Afraid of Virginia Woolf?* could be interpreted as meaning 'lowbrows-will-be-persecuted' (Pryce-Jones 1964), and, according to Alan Schneider, that was certainly the impression made on the 'lower middle class friends and relatives of the crew' who made up the preview audience, and were too nervous to laugh. But, Schneider notes with relief, 'sophisticated Londoners, language differences and all, latched onto us no differently than had sophisticated New Yorkers' once the performances proper had started (Schneider 1986: 333).

The reliability of such reports, however, is questionable: other, somewhat contradictory, accounts suggest that audience reaction, like the play itself, was being interpreted according to the particular prejudices of the commentator. For John Chapman, for example, the phenomenon which came as 'a revelation and a shock to me at the

opening of *Who's Afraid'* was not the decadent laughter of the intelligentsia, but the emergence of 'the new female audience', whose
behaviour was anything but sophisticated. In a commentary article
for New York's *Sunday News,* which appeared the week after his initial
Daily News review of *Virginia Woolf'*s premiere, Chapman proposed
that the play was fit 'For Dirty-Minded Females Only':

> while I cringed and shuddered at the most soiled and fruitiest language I
> have yet heard on a stage, the house was echoing with the shrieks and
> guffaws of the 'ladies.' They made such a racket I never did hear any
> men; perhaps the other men, like myself, were more embarrassed than
> amused and therefore kept quiet . . . *Who's Afraid* is merely sensational.
> Ladies, you may have it. Whoop, holler, squeal, yip, shriek and gasp
> deliciously to the content of your dear little hearts. Albee, I fear you are
> a goner. (*Chapman 1962b*)

Similarly misogynistic sentiments recurred elsewhere. Schneider's
touring production was greeted by the Los Angeles *Citizen News* with
the comment that 'the run at the Biltmore should be a successful one
– the women will see to it. It's strictly their cup of tea, and how they
will relish it' (Elgee 1963).

Clearly the play was seen in some quarters as a threat to traditional,
patriarchally ordered gender roles, and there can be little doubt that it
was Albee's depiction of Martha's behaviour which lay behind such
anxieties. This character was the single most shocking aspect of the
play for audiences in the early 1960s. Uta Hagen dominated the stage
of the Billy Rose, all 'gin-fogged mind' and 'profane as a muleskin-
ner' (Chapman 1962a), and although, coming from a male character,
such behaviour would have been far less remarkable, this depiction
broke all precedent in terms of what was deemed 'normal' or acceptable for female characters in Broadway plays. Those critics who felt
obliged to respond to this apparent provocation (and there were
many) attempted to explain Martha away according to one of three
suppositions. The first was that such women might well exist in 'real
life', but that they should certainly not be dignified with representa-

tion on stage, since this could only encourage 'dirty-minded females' of the sort abhorred by Chapman. The second, contradictory perspective viewed the play itself as 'essentially misogynist' (Weatherby 1962), seeing Martha as a vindictive caricature of womanhood, a shrew to be tamed by George in a final showdown which thus acted as wish-fulfilment for the author's fear and hatred of women. Since it was assumed by many that real women in real marriages would never behave that badly, Martha was viewed as a kind of monstrous dual stereotype – both smothering mother and voracious whore. 'Miss Hagen', Walter Kerr wrote, tellingly if unconsciously conflating Martha's language with both castration and fellatio, 'sends the knife of her tongue flicking into Mr. Hill's vitals' (Kerr 1962b).

Unsurprisingly, Albee himself has always insisted that Martha's more outrageous behaviour represents a frustrated and very human response to the circumstances she finds herself in, and he cites the play's popularity with female audiences in support of his point: 'she's a real gutsy three dimensional well rounded woman who can play the monster when she's thrust into that role . . . Usually the men misunderstand; women seem to be a little more tolerant of the women I create, which leads me to suspect they aren't monsters' (Kolin 1988: 87). Such explanations, however, did nothing to stop the spread of the third and most insistent supposition about Martha; namely, that she was not really female at all, but a male character crudely transgendered for the sake of public consumption. Since Albee's homosexuality was an open secret in New York's artistic circles, despite his still being 'in the closet' at this time, a rumour quickly spread that the play was really about a meeting of four gay men, and had been rewritten for its Broadway premiere. This notion of a veiled subtext, incomprehensible to the general public, was leapt on by many as confirmation of the play's underlying decadence and perversity, and as an explanation for its ambiguities, its lack of up-front message.

There is almost nothing in the play itself which could support this 'four homosexuals' interpretation of *Virginia Woolf*, but given the general unwillingness to accept that George and Martha's marriage

could be representative of a real, heterosexual marriage, the reading
had immediate appeal, not least in accounting for the supposedly
masochistic and psychotic nature of the relationship. (At this time,
the American Psychiatric Association still listed homosexuality as a
mental illness.) The allusion to this supposed gay subtext appeared
directly following the Broadway premiere, as part of John Chapman's
attack on 'dirty-minded females' (the mix of misogyny and homo-
phobia here is confused but perhaps not surprising). 'This is, at base,
an arresting drama which would be much better and more tasty
without its Fire Island dressing; but it is the dressing which is attracting the "ladies"' (Chapman 1962b). Fire Island was a local resort
widely known to be popular with New York's gay community, a fact
which suggests that Chapman had more than one sort of 'lady' in
mind. His use of innuendo was necessary because he was clearly
casting aspersions on Albee himself, and at this time publishing propriety forbade explicit reference to the homosexuality of public
figures in the mainstream press (the prejudice that dare not speak its
name). However, Chapman's point was quickly picked up by other
journalists at more reputable newspapers. In April 1963, with the
much-talked-about run of Albee's play still playing to sell-out houses,
New York Times drama critic Howard Taubman wrote a lengthy commentary article claiming to expose the pervasive influence of homosexuality on Broadway 'this season'. Though he mentions no names,
Virginia Woolf is clearly his prime target, and he alludes blatantly to
the play's much-discussed 'themes' in the article's title: 'Modern
Primer: Helpful Hints to Tell Appearances from Truth'. Taubman
offers a series of hints for spotting this theme, in case 'you are so
literal-minded and unsophisticated as to assume that characters and
situations are what they seem', and his checklist of giveaway signs
reads as a catalogue of accusations against Albee's play:

> Look out for the male character who is young, handsome, remote and
> lofty, [and] note whether his very presence tends to make the women he
> encounters . . . instantly into Jezebels . . . Beware the husband who

hasn't touched his wife for years. . . . Look out for the baleful female
who is a libel on womanhood. Look out for the hideous wife who makes
a horror of the marriage relationship . . . Be alert to scabrous innuendo
abut the normal male–female sexual relationship, especially if the
writer is not a filthy-minded hack but one of demonstrated talent . . . If
only we could recover our lost innocence and could believe that people
on the stage are what they are supposed to be! Would that such a miracle
oblige the playwrights obsessed by homosexuality and its problems to
define their themes clearly and honestly. (*Taubman 1963*)

Taubman himself, of course, is hardly dealing 'clearly and honestly'
with his targets here. Around the same time, however, Richard
Schechner published a more direct attack from much the same perspective: 'Albee makes dishonesty a virtue', he insisted in his 1963
TDR editorial on the play: 'We must not ignore what Albee represents and portends, either for our theatre or for our society. The lie of
his work is the lie of our theatre and the lie of America. The lie of
decadence must be fought' (Schechner 1963: 10).

In defence of this extraordinary diatribe, Schechner lists the
aspects of *Virginia Woolf* which he declares himself 'tired' of seeing
in the American theatre, including its 'badly plotted' structure, and
its central dramatic metaphor (the child) which is 'neither philo-
sophically, psychologically, nor poetically valid'. Yet these familiar
dramaturgical objections are hardly civilisation-shattering. The crux
of Schechner's objections clearly lies with his final bullet-point: most
of all he is 'tired of morbidity and sexual perversity which are there
only to titillate an impotent and homosexual theatre and audience.
I'm tired of Albee' (1963: 9). Schechner, like Taubman and
Chapman, avoids actually saying that Albee is gay, but his insinua-
tion is obvious: after all, the commercial Broadway audience was not
generally 'homosexual' any more than homosexuals are generally
impotent. Moreover, Schechner's attack on the fabric of the play is a
catalogue of the stereotypically unmanly, effeminate qualities attributed to homosexuals: 'The values of *Virginia Woolf* are perverse and
dangerous. Self-pity, drooling, womb-seeking weakness' (1963: 8).

The recurrence of such denunciations in other, similar commentary articles, both in *TDR* and elsewhere (see for example Driver 1964; Baxandall 1965; Kaplan 1965; Kauffmann 1966a), suggests that, for many, the success of Albee's play was being interpreted as a threat to the very existence of a healthy, red-blooded American theatre culture.

There can be little doubt that, whatever these critics' intentions, the rumours and denunciations added considerably to the controversy value of the play itself, and thus to its box-office take. The myth of the play's hidden subtext received further reinforcement during 1963 and 1964 as the press periodically reported such dubious stories as movie star Kim Stanley's claim that she was turned down for the role of Martha in the London production because she was too feminine (Hagen's defining performance had been widely seen as very 'masculine' in its force and tone). A questionable *New York Times* report even quoted Ingmar Bergman as saying that he had considered using an all-male cast for his 1963 Stockholm production: 'I wish I had dared' (quoted Gottfried 1967: 266). Whether Bergman or, more likely, the reporter was suffering from misapprehensions about the play is unclear, but the persistence of such stories must have been a contributory factor in casting decisions for the film version. There is little wonder that Warner Brothers did not pursue Albee's preferred option of Bette Davis for the role of Martha, given that she was well known to be a camp icon among gay men. Instead, Ernest Lehman's decision to cast Elizabeth Taylor meant that, even artificially aged, she carried along with her well-established connotations of ultimate feminine beauty. Adding her real-life husband, Richard Burton, to the mix further guaranteed that this would be seen as an authentically heterosexual pairing. Such concerns also perhaps help to account for the appearance in the screenplay of a few lines which Albee did not write, but which (in notable contradiction of Mike Nichols' 'ethical' refusal to titillate audiences) smack of determinedly heterosexual locker-room banter. Lehman's deletion of George and Nick's exchange on 'gangles' of geese, for example, was covered in the screenplay by the insertion of a quite unnecessary piece of smut (Albee's original words are those without emphasis): 'The way to a man's heart, *the wide inviting avenue,* is through his wife's belly, and don't you forget it'; '*And I'll bet your wife's got the widest, most inviting avenue on the whole damn campus.*'

Despite such modifications, however, *Newsweek* magazine used its review of the film to cut through the veil of allusion created by the mainstream press, publishing the most virulently explicit condemnation of *Virginia Woolf* yet to appear in print:

> Albee is using his harrowing heterosexual couples as surrogates for homosexual partners having a vicious, narcissistic, delightedly self-indulgent spat. He has not really written about men and women, with a potential for love and sex, however withered the potential may be. He has written about saber-toothed humans who cannot reproduce, and who need to draw buckets of blood before they can feel compassion for each other. (*Newsweek 1966*)

What seems most striking about this passage is not so much the critic's inflammatory language as the fact that it can be trotted out so casually; taken as read. Clearly this interpretation had acquired the spurious legitimacy of common sense during the few years since John Chapman's initial, coded allusion to Fire Island. Albee himself was so appalled by the *Newsweek* review that he wrote a letter of protest: he received a reply from the critic which stated, in effect, that 'seeing the play as being about four homosexuals was the only way that he could live with [it]' (Kolin 1988: 53). Albee recounted this incident in an interview for the Fall 1966 edition of the literary journal. *Paris Review,* in which – stung by the film reviews – he made his first public response to the suggestions that the characters in *Virginia Woolf* were really men. He was careful to point out that, even if he had changed his characters' sexes, this would be a legitimate creative decision: 'only the most callow or insecure or downright stupid critic would fault Proust's work, for example, for the transposition that he made of characters' sexes'. Nevertheless, he stressed, 'the facts are simple: *Who's Afraid of Virginia Woolf?* was written about two heterosexual couples. If I had wanted to write a play about four homosexuals, I would have done so' (Kolin 1988: 52–3).

In point of fact, such a play does exist: among Albee's early, unpublished manuscripts is a handwritten piece dating from 1951, titled *Ye Watchers and Ye Lonely Ones*, which depicts two hustlers who try to convince themselves that they are not the same way inclined as their customers, and a male May-to-December couple breaking up amid mutual recriminations. Both scenarios are handled with a remarkable subtlety and compassion for the characters, and not a trace of 'drooling self-pity'. For the most part, though, Albee's sexuality has not been a concern of his writing. The more significant autobiographical threads of Albee's work, as Doric Wilson points out, relate to his family background as an adoptive child: 'All of Edward's plays are about children and parents, they're not about [sexual] relationships.' Both couples in *Virginia Woolf* are deeply traumatised by their inability to conceive and raise children – a factor which, obviously, affects straight couples very differently than it does gay ones. For women in particular, in the pre-feminist era when Albee wrote the play, childlessness was a considerable social stigma, simply because motherhood was treated as the one true, legitimate function of adult life. For Doric Wilson, author of such 'out' gay plays as *Street Theater* (a satire on the Stonewall Riots of 1969), the emotional subtext of *Virginia Woolf* is indisputably indicative of such heterosexual trauma, playing as it does on the desperation of barrenness: 'I've discussed this with Uta, I've discussed it with Stritch: it's that third act speech of Martha's that nails forever the idea that it's a fag part – "we take our tears and we freeze them" – the clink clink speech. That is a woman's speech. That is not a drag queen speech or a transvestite speech, that's a woman's speech.' Nevertheless, such was the weight of the fear and rumour surrounding the play in the 1960s that even the absence of offspring was taken as evidence of disguised deviance. 'The reason George and Martha cannot have children is because they are really men – homosexuals', wrote newspaper critic Martin Gottfried in his 1967 publication, *A Theater Divided*: 'George and and Martha (and even Nick and Honey) are about as heterosexual as Mutt and Jeff' (266–7).

By the late 1960s, such assumptions had been so frequently repeated that they had acquired the spurious validity of 'known fact', and had for many become an integral part of the experience of viewing the play. Reviewing the Atelje 212 production at Lincoln Center in 1968, for example, the critic for *Women's Wear Daily* first expounded on how this very physical performance had enabled a reconsideration of the play, before continuing with a plea for another new variation: 'perhaps Mr. Albee would [now] agree to a production of his original four-man homosexual version. Would it work? Yes!' (P.D.D.) Two years later, in November 1970, *Variety* took this nonsense to another level by printing a front-page story announcing that Henry Fonda and Richard Burton were planning to star in a new Broadway production, with support from Warren Beatty and Jon Voight as Nick and Honey. Fonda and Burton, it was reported, had taken the idea to Richard Barr, who had been enthusiastic, but Albee was less keen. Barr promptly responded with a letter to *Variety* rubbishing the story and protesting its 'damaging' insinuations: 'That "Albee flatly refused to permit it" suggests that there was a conversation about it. That "the project was conceived by Fonda and Burton" is also untrue as Mr. Fonda confirmed to me. There were no plans, there were no conversations' (Barr 1970). *Variety* refused to apologise for the story, maintaining that a representative for Fonda and Burton had confirmed its veracity – though they did not venture to suggest whether it was Burton or Fonda who wished to play Martha! Barr and Albee subsequently ensured that a clause was added to the contracts for both professional and amateur performing rights, which stipulated that all the roles must be played by actors of the prescribed gender.

SHIFTING PARADIGMS

By the 1970s, the gay liberation movement was under way, and changing attitudes to homosexuality have, mercifully, diminished both the incidence and the virulence of the questions surrounding the 'true' gender and sexuality of Albee's characters (a peculiar idea in itself; as if they had some life beyond the play as written). What has emerged, instead, is the more sophisticated awareness that the play, though dealing with two straight couples, is nevertheless informed by what might now be called the 'gay sensibility' of its author. Albee, for example, like Tennessee Williams, queers the heterosexist construction of conventional drama by presenting an Adonis-like male figure (Nick), rather than a desirable female, as the object of the play's erotic gaze (such as it is). In this respect, at least, Martha – as the character who is most loudly fascinated by Nick's 'potential' – can be read as enunciating a gay male perspective (though this interest is, of course, also plausible coming from a heterosexual female). A gay sensibility is also evident in the play's occasionally campy wit, usually expressed in incidental turns of phrase such as George's reference to 'Christ and all those girls' (87). Moreover, former friends of Albee's, such as gay playwright Robert Heide, have confirmed that some of George and Martha's repartee was lifted almost verbatim from Albee's own, sometimes bitter, exchanges with his lover of the time, Bill Flanagan. This is 'a heterosexual union which sometimes seems like a parody of a bickering gay relationship', Paul Taylor suggested in his *Independent* review of the 1996 Almeida revival: 'Martha's first speech is about Bette Davis, for God's sake' (*LTR* 1996: 1232).

In his critical history of homosexual drama in America, *Acting Gay*, John Clum provides an intriguing analysis of George and Martha's theatricalised banter as 'an exercise in camp', by stressing the connection – now well established in queer theory – between gay experience and self-conscious performativity (Clum 1992: 188). Since homosexuals have traditionally been faced with the choice either of 'passing for straight' by performing silence and remaining closeted, or with stressing their difference by performing some degree of deviance from the 'norm', there has always been a greater degree of theatrical artifice in gay life than in the supposedly 'natural' behaviour of the heterosexual majority. Hence, Clum suggests, the evident delight in performativity evinced by George and Martha, who even refer to their imaginary child scenario as 'the bit' – theatrical slang for a short skit or comedy routine. Clum is not, it should be noted, the first to make such connections: it was the overt theatricality of much gay culture which lay behind Stanley Kauffmann's 1966 *New York Times* denunciation of Albee, Tennessee Williams and William Inge. 'Three of the most successful playwrights of the last twenty years are (reputed) homosexuals', Kauffmann declares, adopting the same allusive approach as had Howard Taubman three years earlier, before listing many of the same 'telltale signs' of 'disguised gay influence' as had his colleague (Kauffmann 1966a). Writing shortly prior to the release of the film version of *Virginia Woolf*, Kauffmann goes on to suggest – in distinctly pejorative terms – that

> Homosexual artists . . . glorif[y] their exclusion. They exalt style, manner, surface . . . because these elements of art, at which they are often adept, are legal tender in their transactions with the world . . . What is more, this [approach is] an instrument of revenge on the main body of society. Theme and subject are important historical principles in our art. The arguments to prove that they are of diminishing importance – in fact, ought never to have been important – are cover for an attack on the idea of social relevance. By adulation of sheer style, this group tends . . . to reduce art to a clever game that society cannot keep them from playing.

The implication is, of course, that society *should* stop 'them'. Kauffmann's argument seeks to outlaw as 'queer' and morally unserious any attempt to reflect aesthetically on the uncertainties and ambiguities of contemporary life. As John Clum puts it, 'Albee's plays are interesting because they question the very assumptions of naturalism – rationality, the belief in a "truth" one can grasp', and yet 'critics tied this skepticism . . . to Albee's sexuality in ways which denied him anything but his homosexuality' (Clum 1992: 183).

Moreover, while overt performativity of the type displayed in *Virginia Woolf* may well be characteristic of 'the gay writer's ambivalence' toward conventional realism (Clum 1992: 185), such strategies are by no means exclusively related to an artist's sexuality. Indeed, in a late twentieth-century culture dominated by image, style and ubiquitous performance, and by the attendant inaccessibility of stable truths, it has become almost standard to adopt a sceptical, relativistic perspective on contemporary experience. With the benefit of hindsight, it is possible to see that the threat which traditional liberal humanists like Kauffmann glimpsed in Albee's work in the 1960s was – in their own terms – a very real one. The days when plays boasted neatly resolved 'theme and subject', when moral seriousness could be presented without some degree of self-consciously ironic performativity, were numbered. ('Irony may be the only way we *can* be serious today', Linda Hutcheon has commented: 'There is no innocence in our world' [Hutcheon 1988: 39].) In short, Kauffmann and other doom-sayers had misdiagnosed the threat; what they detected in *Virginia Woolf* was not so much the homosexual perversion of heterosexual culture as the creeping advent of postmodernity. This is not to suggest that the play itself is 'postmodernist' as such, but that it looks forward to the attendant uncertainties of much that *could* be classifiable under that term – a term which for many is integrally related to the ubiquity of 'language games' and 'performance-related' assessments of everyday behaviour. 'The metaphor of the dramaturgical society, or "life as theater" has now become interactional reality', writes Norman Denzin: 'Art not only mirrors life, it structures and reproduces it. The postmodern society is a dramaturgical society' (Denzin 1991: x). George and Martha's vertiginous, self-creating game-playing stood, in the early 1960s, at the thin end of an historically inevitable wedge.

It was a review of the film version of *Virginia Woolf* which first articulated the significance of the play's performativity by drawing connections with another recent movie of groundbreaking importance. 'Albee has been congratulated for salvaging true theatre out of naturalism,' Ernest Callenbach wrote in *Film Quarterly*,

> but it seems to me his chief contribution has been to reintroduce a spirit of theatrical 'games' . . . What is most intriguing about *Virginia Woolf* is that it does on the stage something like what [Alain] Resnais did in [his 1961 film, *Last Year at*] *Marienbad*: it presents a fabric of speeches . . . in which we cannot tell how much is 'real' . . . By the end of the play, when we see the tortuous extent to which their games can go, we know, looking back, that nothing they have said can be taken for granted. (*Callenbach 1966: 45–6*)

This perspective had been unthinkable to theatre reviewers, flying as it does in the face of every assumption about naturalistic drama's gradual revelation the 'truth' of the situation presented. By 1976, however, when Albee directed his own revival of *Virginia Woolf*, Callenbach's realisation that the play's importance might lie in this embracing of existential uncertainty had finally begun to be appreciated more widely. 'Albee's production seems to stress the characters' living in this gray area between truth/reality and lie/illusion,' wrote Robb Baker in the *Soho Weekly News*, 'so that we're never quite sure about anything they do or say – almost any line, any reference, any attitude in the play might be a false one.' Howard Kissel of *Women's Wear Daily* made much the same point, linking it explicitly to a change in perspective facilitated by time: 'Because we are now familiar with the play, and, even more important, because we have learned that you can't make such neat distinctions between what is real and what is not, we can now enjoy watching Martha and George deliberately inventing fictions for themselves and their guests.' This lack of firm grounding for the audience, he concluded, generates 'just as much drama' as the older mechanics of truth-revealing plot, and – paradoxically – 'perhaps even a more truthful drama'.

What, one might ask, were the lessons 'learned' since 1962 that made such ideas thinkable by 1976? On a global scale, the obvious factor was America's loss of complacency about its own basic decency: after the long nightmare of Vietnam, the unanswered questions surrounding the Kennedy and King assassinations, the revelations over Watergate and so forth, the average citizen was far better prepared to believe that nothing was necessarily what it seemed, and that manipulative words could mask any number of deceptions and counter-truths. Several reviewers of Albee's revival were quick to point out other ways in which the cultural context had changed: 'Since marital breakups have become commonplace,' wrote *Variety's* Bone, 'perhaps the behind-the-scenes exploration of one of the causes of estrangement [i.e. childlessness] may be even more significant than the first time around.' For *New York* reviewer Alan Rich, Albee's characters seemed much more familiar and relevant in the current climate than previously: 'Every educated person will recognize in [Martha] at least one quintessential campus wife of his own acquaintance. Since 1962, she will have watched campus life torn apart by Vietnam and Kent State, and signed petitions against food additives. These have made her harder than the Martha of 1962 and, because she *is* that Martha, all the hollower inside.'

There had also been enormous changes in American theatre in the years between the two Broadway productions, changes which Michael Smith's original *Village Voice* review, praising Albee's play as a theatrical turning-point, had foreseen with almost uncanny prescience. His references to the impact of the play's sheer relentlessness, and to Albee substituting 'a kind of ritual' for linear dramaturgy, now reads as a precursor to the development later in the 1960s of all kinds of experiments in ritualism, sensory disorientation and quasi-Artaudian 'cruelty'. By the time *Virginia Woolf* was revived in Chicago in September 1970, *Sun Times* critic Glenna Syse could reasonably remark that, in the eight years since the play's Broadway premiere, 'theater has changed perhaps more than it did in the 50 years previous'. But for all Smith's anticipation of the agenda of 1960s theatrical experiment, the most crucial insight in his review lay in his emphasis on *Virginia Woolf* being 'first of all a real play', in the sense of reinventing a set of already-existing conventions: 'Edward Albee has found fire in the soggy ashes of naturalism and forged a technique of inestimable potential. This is a crucial event in the birth of a contemporary American theatre' (Michael Smith 1962: 17). It took time for that prophecy to be fulfilled, of course: the chaos of the 1960s had to blow over before many of America's young playwrights were prepared to look seriously again at realistic drama. The 1970s, however, saw the emergence of what William Demastes has labelled a 'new realism', in the work of dramatists as diverse as David Mamet, Sam Shepard, Marsha Norman and Maria Irene Fornes. In all these cases, the old clockworks of naturalism were rejected. As playwright David Rabe put it, 'that form which thinks that cause and effect are proportionate and clearly apparent, that people know what they are doing as they do it . . . that one thing leads to another in a rational, mechanical way' seemed dated and inappropriate: he and his contemporaries were seeking instead to evoke something of 'the powerful sweeps of pattern and energy that is our lives' (quoted Demastes 1988: 2).

Perhaps the best evidence of just how far the theatrical goalposts had moved by the mid-1970s was the Broadway production of David Mamet's *American Buffalo*, which opened just a few months after Albee's revival, in February 1977. Mamet's play was condemned by several critics in terms alarmingly similar to those used in relation to Albee's, fifteen years previously. Mamet's first play to appear on Broadway was, much like *Virginia Woolf*, a single-set, small-cast drama which appeared realistic on the surface, but with a plot which turns out – in the final scene – to be a house of cards built on a lie. If some critics had felt tricked by *Virginia Woolf* in 1962, it took Mamet's upping of the same stakes to infuriate opinion now; that and a use of rhythmic profanity which made Albee's play look like a model of propriety. Mamet, of course, acknowledges Albee as one of his key influences: Michael Smith's prophecy was finally coming true, as Albee's unorthodox appropriation of realism provided the inspiration for others to pursue still further his rejection of linear, revelatory logic.

Paradoxically, the American audience's greater familiarity with, and toleration for, material dominated by the manipulation of deceptive appearances also meant that spectators at the 1976 revival of *Virginia Woolf* seemed better prepared to see *beyond* its surfaces. The bitterly cynical sense of humour which had shocked and alienated many when the play premiered now appeared much more comprehensible, while the diminution in shock value allowed observers to see past the pyrotechnics of George and Martha's battles to the profound bond between them. Julius Novick's *Village Voice* review, for example, remarked pointedly that the intensity of George and Martha's relationship suggests 'an integrity that is absent in Nick and Honey, who pick their way through life, carefully avoiding commitment. [*Virginia Woolf* now] seems to be primarily about . . . the variety, the complexity, the paradoxes, of which love is capable – about the terrible things that people can do to one another and still, God help us, be lovers.'

Novick's perspective was noticeably more in step with that of his fellow critics than Smith's *Voice* piece had been in 1962. Of course there were still a few insisting on the sacredness of the old mechanics: Edwin Wilson of the *Wall Street Journal* and Martin Gottfried of the *New York Post* were still determined to demonstrate the manifest inadequacies of the play's plot and themes. They were, however, firmly in the minority, and even Gottfried now had to acknowledge that his 'Mutt and Jeff' comments of 1967 were misplaced: 'For all the bitchy cruelty in the exchanges between George and Martha . . . there is a real marriage presented here; a believably male–female marriage and one relating to all marriages.' If that seems like a radical turnaround, perhaps still more revealing was the change of heart by Walter Kerr, who had so assiduously critiqued the flaws of the third act in 1962. Now writing for the *New York Times*, he praised the play's steady 'building up [of] the inexplicit, the ambiguous, the unreal', to the point that, with George's revelation of the death of the imagined son, 'we believe – believe that what is not happening is in some sense happening; believe in an emptiness between George and Martha that required the invention of a son; believe in the necessity of the child's death if the terrifying emptiness, filled only with violently exact speech, is to be ended.'

As was noted in chapter one, one of Albee's major concerns in directing this production had been to convince his audience of the 'plausibility' of precisely the events that Kerr outlines. Yet Albee himself insists that, in practical terms, the 1976 performance was 'very little different' from that of 1962, and that personally he had had no trouble seeing in Schneider's production the merits which the critics had belatedly discovered in his. For Albee, the change in critical perspective had a very simple explanation: 'The play had developed an almost infallible reputation by [1976]. When people see things a second time around – it comes with a reputation.' That reputation has only acquired further armour-plating in the ensuing decades: indeed the reviews of the London productions of 1981, 1987 and 1996 demonstrate a steady decline in the number of critics willing to poke holes in the play. Even in 1996, of course, there were still those bemoaning its failings. *The Spectator's* Sheridan Morley even criticised the play's length in terms which implied this was a new complaint: 'the years are beginning to make [*Virginia Woolf*] look a little repetitive and, at more than three hours with two intervals, [it is] sometimes unnecessarily circular' (*LTR* 1996: 1227). On the other hand, though, *Evening Standard* columnist Nicholas de Jongh announced, with equal obliviousness to the irony involved, that 'the shocking, climactic scene when the husband brings the dream of parenthood to a deathly finale comes across as one of the defining moments in modern theatre' (*LTR* 1996: 1230).

This acceptance of the play's classic status, however, should not go unqueried, for it seems to have been made possible by the now widespread acceptance of an overly neat interpretative reading. De Jongh, for example, explained that the 'defining moment' of that climactic scene presents 'an image of the grief caused when people are forced to face up to hard reality'. In his *Guardian* review of the Almeida production, Michael Billington concurred that 'George and Martha finally acknowledge the need to swap illusion for reality' (*LTR* 1996: 1231). This notion that the play offers a neat binary divide and an implicit choice – between living with illusion or living with 'truth' – bears little or no relation to what actually happens on stage. It does, however, have the great advantage of rendering the play safely explicable, and over the years it has acquired virtually cast-iron currency through repetitions of precisely this sort. And although the critics who initially offered this reading thought of it as trite, and blamed Albee, those who now repeat it – with mantra-like predictability in reviews of every new production – take as read its profundity. Much the same is true of the regularity with which reviewers now trot out the assumption that Albee's play – thanks to its characters' names, the name of the college town, and the fact that George throws Spengler's book across the room – is an allegory about 'the Decline of the West'. In his 1996 review, Michael Billington extended this reading to the point of offering a new take on the old comparison between *Virginia Woolf* and *Long Day's Journey into Night*, suggesting that Albee's might well be 'the greater play' on the grounds that, where 'O'Neill dramatises his own family's tribulations, [Albee] puts on stage a much larger slice of his scarred and fatigued Republic' (*LTR* 1996: 1231). The logic here is a little fuzzy.

Occasionally, of course, somebody tries to query – with more or less articulacy – the set of questionable orthodoxies now surrounding *Who's Afraid of Virginia Woolf?* In a commentary piece on the Almeida production for the London *Daily Telegraph*, Susan Crosland (1996) complained that 'I see no reason to go along with Albee's theme that we must strip away *all* illusions if we are to reach reality . . . Has any good relationship ever survived total candour at every single moment of the day? The mind boggles.' Crosland pointedly confesses that 'I didn't think of Albee's vaunted theme' when actually watching the play's climax; yet since everybody apparently knows that this is what the play is 'about', she does not interrogate this realisation further. Instead, she sets her sights on challenging the 'widely held view' that *Virginia Woolf* demonstrates how 'intimacy between [men and women] leads inevitably to their savaging each other'. Thirty-five years on, it seems, the play was still a perverse slur on the institution of marriage, 'the cornerstone of our culture. . . . What is the evidence that power struggles are peculiar to heterosexual intimacy? . . . Albee's first version of the play was said to be about a homosexual couple.' Crosland's article unwittingly demonstrates the extent to which the actual script of *Who's Afraid of Virginia Woolf?* is now but one of many, accumulated layers of cultural 'textuality' which are brought into play whenever a new production is mounted.

CHAPTER 3

'THE EXORCISM': GETTING THE WORST OUT OF YOUR PERFORMERS

In this final chapter, we turn to a detailed discussion of the relative merits of several different performances of *Who's Afraid of Virginia Woolf?* The first point to stress in any such discussion is that the distinctions between productions are, in many respects, necessarily minimal: Albee's masterfully orchestrated, heavily annotated script provides a very coherent impression of how the play is to appear on stage, and the options for interpretative variation are thus kept tightly delimited. Albee himself, moreover, continues to stipulate that all productions must perform the text in its entirety without cuts or any other form of 'adaptation', however subtle. He has always maintained that the playwright's is the single most important creative voice at work in any production, and that this authority may not be questioned by anyone other than himself. 'I can be severe with my own text. I'll cut it if it doesn't work', he has said of his own experiences directing his plays: 'But I won't let another director do it' (Drake 1989: 4).

This attitude does not, perhaps, sit well with contemporary notions of theatre production as an art form which enables a collaborative interplay of multiple creative voices. Nevertheless, it would be misleading to conclude that Albee maintains such tight control over his work simply for control's sake. Indeed, actors who have worked with him as director often stress the unusual degree of freedom he gives them in finding their own way into their roles. Colleen Dewhurst, for example, describes him as 'always compassionate, allowing us free rein to try different things', during rehearsals for the 1976 revival of *Virginia Woolf* (Dewhurst 1997: 244). When once asked whether, as a director, he stages his plays according to some particular blueprint in his head, Albee replied simply that

I don't care so much about staging. If somebody's going to be on stage, I want them on stage; if they're going to exit, I want them to leave; if they're going to be dead, I want them not wandering around. I don't write down at the first draft of every play exactly how many steps one moves – that's got to be fairly fluid and make sense. I always tell actors, whenever I direct, 'You can do anything you want, as long as you end up with exactly what *I* want.' (*Samuels 1994*)

That last sentence sums up the paradox of presenting Albee's plays on stage, and *Who's Afraid of Virginia Woolf?* in particular. The author's intentions are so strongly apparent in his text that one could not avoid them if one wanted to. Yet even if these are observed to the letter, there is still a great deal of scope for finding individual interpretations of the material, particularly for actors. Albee's strongest objections have always been directed toward attempts by directors and designers to impose their own ideas on his work from the outside, rather than exploring the text from the 'inside'. As I will seek to demonstrate, the most complete and satisfying productions of *Who's Afraid of Virginia Woolf?* have been those which have most rigorously investigated the subtleties of the text, and have been most careful to avoid imposing prior assumptions as to how it should be presented.

FRAMING THE PERFORMANCE

The first, and in many ways the most powerful statement made by any production about its approach to a play is apparent in the visual design of the setting. The design frames the whole of the performance, constantly providing certain basic sign information to the audience which fundamentally colours its reception of the play, and Albee – knowing this full well – has very clear ideas about what is and is not appropriate for *Who's Afraid of Virginia Woolf?* His stage directions state only that 'the scene is the living room of a house on the campus of a small New England college' – a description that might be regarded as sufficiently sketchy to permit some degree of interpretative licence in its visualisation. However, Albee is adamant that the description be taken entirely literally, and that the set create as straight an illusion of this 'reality' as possible:

> I don't like sets that make comments, and a naturalistic play should not have a set that makes comments. I mean there's no such thing as a naturalistic play, but *Virginia Woolf* comes fairly close, and I don't want a fucking symbolic set! I don't want a set to tell me how to react to the play! The set is the container for the thing contained.

A strictly naturalistic set will, of course, tell an audience 'how to react' as surely as will something more 'symbolic'. Albee's intention, it seems, is for an audience to be 'told' to view *Virginia Woolf*'s characters as ordinary people in an ordinary environment. Yet that attitude has, from the play's inception, set him somewhat at odds with many of its directors and designers. Alan Schneider, for example, perceived the play not as naturalism but as a greatly heightened drama built on a foundation of realism, a confrontation of almost mythic proportions: 'In rehearsal, I would tell the actors that they were not in a realistic play – otherwise they'd all be flat on the floor [in a drunken stupor]. These are not little people but giants battling on a cliff' (Schneider 1986: 310). Schneider was initially intent on having a stylised setting which reflected this vision, but Albee insisted that the illusion of an actual living-room was paramount. Designer William Ritman took these demands on board and created a claustrophobically enclosed domestic environment, using comparatively low wall flats and – unusually for the period – a looming, angled ceiling. This was 'a realistic set that suggested both a cave and a womb' (Schneider 1986: 317).

Albee was happy with this approach, but is prone to complain when such balancing-act designs become even slightly more suggestive than this. The setting for the 1996 Almeida/Aldwych production, for example, designed by John Napier (also responsible for such

West End blockbusters as *Starlight Express*), had wall flats loaded with bookshelves but interspersed these with gaps opening out on to a great, dark forest behind. To my mind this effectively evoked the literary tradition of New England's forests standing in for the looming terrors of the unconscious or the unknown. Albee, however, hated it: 'it was the set designer showing off. Set designers show off a lot in Britain these days.' If the walls are to be taken out, he says, they should be taken out altogether (as they were for some of the shorter engagements of the 1963–4 tour): 'I've seen productions where the walls are just indicated; you lose some of the claustrophobia, but. You can do anything you like as long as it doesn't intrude.' Much the same goes for the play's lighting, which Albee does not get involved with unless it draws attention to itself. He tells, hilariously, of an incident during rehearsals for his own 1990 production in Houston:

> I was sitting there in the third act looking at the first technical rehearsal, and I noticed that the quality of light had changed greatly. I called the lighting designer aside and said, 'you're having trouble with the electrics in the theatre, aren't you?' He said 'what do you mean?' I said, 'the lights seem to be dimming and then coming back up again. This obviously means you're either having trouble with the electrics, or someone on the lighting board has made a terrible mistake, because I don't see anybody having lowered or turned a lamp higher for this to have happened.' He looked at me like I was crazy. So I looked at him like he was crazy. I said, 'Don't *help*.'

There have, of course, been productions which have opted for a more stylised presentation than Albee would approve – particularly in Europe. Ingmar Bergman, for example, attempted to impose a stark, monochromatic flavour on his 1963 production, reminiscent of his own black-and-white films: 'one saw only an uncompromisingly bare gray room that consisted of a primitive wall-screen at the back and an absolute minimum of furnishings'. According to Per Erik Wahlund in *Svenska Dagbladet*, '[Bergman's] entire objective has been to enclose and transfix – in a milieu of rat-gray furniture and dishcloth-colored cretonne covers – a model marriage of hatred and humiliation, a relentless battle of the sexes' (Marker and Marker 1982: 52). The first Polish production, in Gdansk in 1965, went still further. 'There is no attempt to reproduce an American professor's living room', noted critic Elizabeth Pond: 'The setting is stark. A hook hangs symbolically from the center ceiling. On the back wall is a surrealistic picture painted for the play by one of Poland's top artists. At stage front is an old-fashioned and marvelously involute rocking chair in which George wraps himself most expressively in the course of the play' (Pond 1965).

These versions, in attempting to capture visually the quality of 'Walpurgisnacht' (or witches' sabbath) suggested by the play's text, might well have pleased Harold Clurman, whose scathing review of the original production suggested that 'a less naturalistic production' might have benefited the play, since '*Who's Afraid of Virginia Woolf?* verges on a certain expressionism, and a production with a touch of that sort of poetry, something not so furiously insistent on the "honesty" of the materials, might give the play some of the qualities I feel it now lacks' (Clurman 1962: 79). Tellingly, though, Clurman's comments are based on an apparent discomfort with the play's refusal to fit neatly into one or other generic category (naturalism, expressionism, absurdism). An alternative diagnosis might be that the play's impact on its audience, its performative force, stems in large part from precisely that disjuncture between its mundane surface and its terrifying undercurrents, a disjuncture which would be obscured or lost in a more stylised presentation. Certainly for Nancy Meckler, director of the 1981 National Theatre production, *Virginia Woolf* relies heavily for its impact on being staged as *unremarkably* as possible – and this despite the fact that her trademark approach is to draw out the expressionistic or surreal aspects of whatever material she is working with. She draws a connection here with Sam Shepard's *True West* (1980) – which she has also directed – in which the stage directions explicitly warn against stylised presentation. This, she notes, is not because Shepard (who had never before written a play with such a detailed set description) had suddenly turned into a conventional playwright, but because the play's surreal qualities, and indeed its wild humour, emerge most effectively by being presented 'straight'. Much the same, she says, is true of *Virginia Woolf*:

> I think you have to direct it totally naturalistically but you need to understand it expressionistically. As with Shepard I do think you need quite a naturalistic set in order for the strangeness to come out. If you put it in a strange situation, you can heighten the meaning but I think you also lose the humour. A lot of the reason audiences laugh is because it looks totally naturalistic, but the people do and say the most outrageous things. In *True West*, it wouldn't be amazing to have twelve toasters on an abstract set, but if you're on a real set it can be hysterical.

Interestingly, one reviewer of Meckler's own production picked up on precisely this point. Writing in the *Financial Times*, Michael Coveney commented that 'Tanya McCallin's set and Lindy Hemming's costumes give the evening the necessary realistic solidity without which such bizarre notions as "humping the hostess" and "getting the guests" would not pack the right punch' (*LTR* 1981: 441). By way of contrast, it is worth noting that the more stylised Swedish and Polish productions cited above were not thought to be particularly funny or entertaining. Their emphasis on the play's darkly nightmarish aspects, at the expense of the kind of disorientating humour emphasised by Meckler, is no doubt in large part a result of the translation process. The kind of verbal witticisms and irony on which Albee's script is built are notoriously difficult to render effectively in a different language, as is clearly indicated by the various Slavic versions of the play's title – from *We Are Not Afraid of the Wolf* to *Who's Afraid of Franz Kafka?*

If Meckler is right, it becomes clear that Albee's objections to the imposition of overt director/designer 'concepts' are far from being simply a case of the writer insisting on ultimate creative authority. It is, it seems, in the best interests of any production to ensure that the play is framed as 'conventionally' as possible. Yet this is not to say that the creativity of a production team need be stifled, simply carefully channelled. There is scope, after all, for a great deal of subtlety within a (quasi-)naturalistic set design. William Ritman's original setting was praised by *Variety* for the way it 'suggest[ed] professional surface and sinister undercurrent' (Hobe 1962), and Lee Baxandall observed that a certain semiotic tension was built into the choice of materials and ornamental features: 'early American period furniture, oak beams, a wrought-iron colonial eagle, an American flag queerly reversed . . . the comforts of modern living side by side with rough-hewn tokens of the revolutionary past, but dominating them: an American House of Intellect' (Baxandall 1965: 30–1). Alan Schneider further notes that the set had 'all kinds of angles and planes that you wouldn't ordinarily have, and strong distortions' (Schechner 1965: 146). Ritman himself has spoken of how he attempted in his design to juxtapose a certain warmth – suggested by the wood hues used in the on-set bookcases and furniture – with the cooler qualities of the green chosen for the wallpaper. 'I didn't want it to look romantic or sentimental. There was a kind of tidiness to the green – it wasn't a green green' (cited McNally 1982: 12). The almost subliminal atmospheric impact of these choices was also intriguingly juxtaposed with a kind of ultra-realism created by the use of an actual clock on stage, which kept real time (albeit set several hours later than the hour at which the audience was watching the play), and the decision to fill the bookshelves with real books rather than using the artificial spine façades which were then still common in the theatre (many of these books were brought in by Schneider from his personal library). The setting thus mirrored directly the tension implicit in the play between the mundanely realistic façade and the heightened atmospherics. For Albee's 1976 revival, which Ritman again designed, a similar balance was achieved by different methods: responding to the different fashions of the 1970s, Ritman this time used wooden panelling across the walls, exposed floorboards, and a bare board door to suggest the hermeti-

7. George Grizzard as Nick, with Uta Hagen and Arthur Hill. Note here the 'cave-like' or 'womb-like' effect created by Ritman's 1962 setting, with its looming ceiling.

cally enclosed atmosphere of a frontier cabin – even as the rows of bookshelves simultaneously bespoke the weight of 'civilisation'.

The most radical variation which can be applied to the staging of *Virginia Woolf*, without actually breaking out of the realistic illusion, is of course the arrangement of the stage–audience relationship. Though Albee prefers the full façade offered by traditional proscenium arch staging, he has no objection in principle to thrust staging or indeed theatre-in-the-round, provided it is not seen to be making a statement: 'I generally don't, in a naturalistic play, like to the see the audience through the actresses' legs. But I've directed in the round. It's OK.' Certainly the periodic attempts to stage *Virginia Woolf* with the audience encompassing some or all of the stage have been met favourably by critics. 'With the Ivanhoe's arena staging', the *Chicago Daily News* declared of George Keathley's highly praised 1970 off-Loop revival, 'the living room of George and Martha has now become a cockpit, or a boxing ring, where blood sports and deadly games are

8. David Suchet as George, Lloyd Owen as Nick, and Clare Holman as Honey in the 1996 Almeida Theatre production, London. The emphasis on early 1960s period design is particularly evident here in the cut of Owen's suit.

performed to the amusement and fascination of spectators' (Christiansen 1970). Similar comments were made of the 1974 Arena Stage production in Washington DC, and of David Thacker's Young Vic version in London in 1987: 'the audience surround the centrally positioned stage as though at a boxing match: a particularly appropriate arrangement for this play' (*LTR* 1987: 186). However, *Punch* critic Robin Ray advised prospective spectators at the Young Vic that, since seating was unreserved, they should aim to 'sit facing the big sofa for the best view of the production' (*LTR* 1987: 187): given the amount of time that characters necessarily spend on that sofa, one wonders if a 360-degree round really is the ideal option for *all* in the theatre.

Another, increasingly important, design question facing producers of *Virginia Woolf* is that of where to *date* the 'naturalism' of the play's action. Written in the early 1960s the play was treated, at first, as entirely contemporary, and the tendency in subsequent decades has been to continue to imply 'the present' by evading the issue of exact era: university professors, after all, are not renowned for their modish sense of style, and it is entirely possible to dress the characters in 'classic' (or just plain dull) outfits which do not suggest the fashions of a particular period. As a result, the most striking visual element of Howard Davies' Almeida production, aside from the looming trees Albee so disliked, was the decision to present the play very clearly as an early 1960s period piece. This choice was most obviously apparent from the characters' clothing (especially the drainpipe cut of Nick's suit) and the profusion of garishly dated rugs and furniture scattered about the set, but this was no mere design whim. For Davies, the early 1960s setting was of central importance to the political metaphor he saw in the play:

> It's very, very important. Edward wrote it in that time and it's a perfect image of that changing world. George and Martha grew up at the end of the New Deal optimism of just before the war, but now there's this younger generation who really haven't found their own voice but in about four, five years time they'll be the generation running things. And they're sort of uncomfortable in the clothes they wear.

In my own experience of watching the production, the discomfort generated by this generation clash seemed almost palpably apparent. The visual period coding established the play as very much a product of the Kennedy era, and the uneasy mixture of hope and cynicism which it generated for many liberals after the conservative hegemony of the 1950s. '*Who's Afraid of Virginia Woolf?* was the result of my examination of the '50s, as much as anything,' Albee has commented: 'Many of us suspected that even though we were terribly enthusiastic about the Thousand Days of Kennedy, before terribly long it would be business as usual and things would slide back to the way they were' (Kolin 1988: 162). In the play, George sees in Nick the embodiment of a newer, more ruthless breed of system-manipulating golden boys, and David Suchet's reading of the part emphasised a bitter, resigned wit which seemed loaded with a sense of the obsolescence of the traditional, liberal values which George himself preaches without necessarily practising. From a historical perspective, though, the early-1960s context was also very suggestive because of the audience's awareness, with hindsight, of the radical social changes which lay just around the temporal corner in the 1960s – the explosion of countercultural dissent, the spectre of Vietnam, the fragmenting of a deceptively homogenous American society into racial, sexual and political interest groups. In Albee's 1976 production, the set and costume design had suggested 1970s styles, and this had no doubt helped prompt the comments of various critics that the characters seemed still more world-weary than they had in 1962, after the cultural chaos of the intervening years. But for a 1990s audience presented with a distinctly 1960s-oriented production design, a different kind of perspective was afforded, with historical resonances and ironies seeming implicit at almost every turn in the action, precisely because the characters (like Albee himself at the time) seem uneasily aware that changes in their world are imminent, but cannot know what form those changes are to take. Even within this microcosm of four 'minor' characters, the sense of a society on the verge of unknown upheavals was powerfully communicated.

The success of Davies' strategy is indicated by the unusual number of critics who picked up on the period echoes in their reviews (even while neglecting to note that it was the design which had triggered such cogitations). '[It] doesn't immediately feel like a Sixties classic. It feels like a Fifties one'; 'It reverberates as a mournful period piece of lost opportunity'; 'a damning verdict on Sixties America as a country whose old ideals had been replaced by rampant materialism' (*LTR* 1996: 1227, 1230). *Time Out* even described Nick and Honey as appearing 'like two characters from a '50s sci-fi movie' – perhaps evoking images of the human automata in *Invasion of the Body Snatchers* (*LTR* 1231). Interestingly, though, Albee himself seems uncomfortable with such readings of the play, insisting that 'I try not to set [my work in] any given time. A play should be able to get by without references to a specific period.' Presumably he is wary of his work coming to be seen as an historical curiosity rather than speaking to the moment. Yet the immediacy of the conflicts between his four characters is never likely to be obscured by the accumulation of other resonances, and the fact remains that the play – thanks to its many references to a war which could only be the Second World War, to George's prohibition-era youth, to divided Berlin, and so on – is as clearly located in its time as is, say, *Death of a Salesman*. Moreover, as all three of the women interviewed for this book (Nancy Meckler, Clare Holman and Albee's producer Elizabeth McCann) were quick to point out, Martha's frustration at having to live *through* her ineffectual husband, and Honey's helpless dependence on Nick, only really make sense coming from women of the generations preceding the (re-)emergence of feminism in the 1970s.

In all likelihood, Howard Davies' production – mounted almost thirty-five years after the original – indicates an approach to the play which will become increasingly common in future, as the circumstances depicted become ever less 'contemporary'. Yet this is in no way to say that its power or relevance will diminish; if *Virginia Woolf* maintains the status of a 'classic', it will be because it is seen to transcend the particularities of the era in which it is set, and speak to people in very different times and places. I would argue, for example,

9. Ben Gazzara as George, Maureen Anderman as Honey, and Colleen Dewhurst as Martha in Albee's own 1976 Broadway production. Ben Gazzara, Maureen Anderman, Colleen Dewhurst. Note William Ritman's 'wood-cabin' style set.

that there was a particular poignancy to the Kennedy-era setting for British audiences in late 1996 and early 1997, just months before a general election in which the Labour Party was likely to unseat the 18-year-old Conservative government. The mixture of hope and cynicism being generated by the modernised, media-friendly 'New Labour' agenda was perhaps not that dissimilar to the public mood to which Albee was responding when he wrote the play in the first place.

CONDUCTING THE PERFORMANCE

If the options for the conceptual framing of *Who's Afraid of Virginia Woolf?* are limited to such questions as the arrangement of stage space, and the degree to which naturalistic or period setting is emphasised, the options for a director's weighting and pacing of the performance itself would initially appear to be similarly restricted. 'No director has tried to superimpose his personality to the extent of doing damage to the clear line of the play,' Albee once observed, before adding pointedly, 'maybe that's because the play has a very clear line' (Stern 1976: 5). His script is indeed very tightly orchestrated, almost musical in its arrangement of the four voices, and thus, for directors of the auteurist persuasion, who like to stamp productions with a distinctive vision of their own, the play is not a particularly attractive option. Indeed Ingmar Bergman, who directed the Swedish premiere in 1963, has gone so far as to suggest that a director is not really necessary at all for *Virginia Woolf,* even for the sake of guiding the pacing of the actors' delivery: 'if they are very good actors, they will find it. They will find a rhythm of their own. I'm sure of that, I am convinced. It's not so difficult. You can read it – and it's all there' (Marker & Marker 1982: 16). Bergman's position is perhaps somewhat extreme, but Nancy Meckler concurs with his basic sentiment: 'he's right in a way, because it is so totally mapped out, and Albee so strongly defines how it should be done that it isn't that interesting to direct, strangely enough. It doesn't need a lot from a director. The actors need encouragement and intelligence but they don't need huge guidance to show them the way.'

As such comments make clear, a great deal of the task of rehearsing *Who's Afraid of Virginia Woolf?* lies simply in the actors' attempts to explore and express the rhythmic qualities which are such an integral part of the characters' verbal fencing. 'I can tell [if it's working] just by walking in on a production, just listening to it,' Albee notes: 'if the rhythms are right, I know that they're playing the roles right.' In the text itself, this authorial sense of musicality is constantly reinforced by italics to indicate where stress is placed, and by bracketed adjectives to suggest the mood the actor is to play. Indeed, these features are so prevalent that some directors and actors have felt an impulse to resist the extent to which the performance is being dictated from the page. 'I hate it,' Uta Hagen noted of Albee's italicising of words: 'for an actor, description of behavior is death. Sometimes I'll have the line retyped so that my visual remembrance isn't influenced by it' (McNally 1982: 22). Clearly, though, Hagen's insistence on a psychological approach to character, in which she builds up an understanding of motivation through internal reference points, is in large part responsible for her objections to such 'external' directions. By contrast, Clare Holman (Howard Davies' Honey) is much more enthusiastic about Albee's directions to actors, since she often prefers to work 'from the outside in', developing a sense of character by internalising the physicality and pacing of the part. Normally, she says, she would resent copious annotation of a part by the author, 'but not in this case. Because every time there was a stage direction and I tried it, it only enhanced it . . . I think the play is a bit like a musical score. He gives you such clear directions that part of you feels like you're playing in an orchestra rather than on a stage. It's a dream to work with, because it's all there to be had.'

With these musical metaphors in mind, and with due respect to Ingmar Bergman, I would argue that the director's role is vital in a production of *Who's Afraid of Virginia Woolf?*, precisely *because* of its tightly scored structure. The director can here be regarded as akin to an orchestra conductor: the notes are all there, but someone has to ensure that the musicians are all playing together to facilitate a coherent interpretation of the material. While the director's staging options may not be as open with this play as with many, any music lover knows that a conductor's interpretation of a score can radically alter its colouring and impact – and that an orchestra without a conductor would be fundamentally lacking in focus. Albee's script may dictate a great deal, but the overall tone of the production, and the choices of which themes and connotations to place particular emphasis on, are left to the director. Moreover, the choreography of the actors in the stage space is left entirely to the director, who needs real skill to ensure that the visual image presented by the play is neither too monotonous (static bodies sitting on furniture), nor gratuitously hyperactive. Alan Schneider once commented that in terms of blocking his actors' movement, this play 'was about the hardest work I've ever done, because there was no indication of it in the script' (Schechner 1965: 146). A cursory examination of critical responses to *Virginia Woolf* bears out just how marked an influence the director provides. Alan Schneider, for example, was highly praised at the time of the original production for his 'almost impossibly sustained direction' (Kerr 1962a); 'an intense level of mutual hatred [is maintained], with slight and brief modulations up and down, clear through to about five minutes before the end. The tones of voice and the actions, the anguishes and the buffooneries, are strung out in perfectly even undulations, like what I imagine to be a banshee wail' (Smith 1962: 17). This sustained pitch, however, also seems to have been responsible for the criticisms which Albee himself received from some critics: 'I'm not sure that he has yet mastered the art of varying the pace over a long period to avoid stretches of monotony' (Weatherby 1962). By contrast, most other major productions have sought to emphasise the play's sense of steady development, of the initially entertaining gradually turning darker, from 'Fun and games' to 'Walpurgisnacht' to 'Exorcism'. For example, Nancy Meckler's 1981 National Theatre production was praised by several critics for the way in which it 'rightly reminds us that Albee builds to his remorseless climax through laughter' (*LTR* 1981: 438). For Meckler herself, the play's sense of gradual intensification seems so obvious that any other approach would be inexplicable: 'It's stages in a fight', she points out, 'I did work on that and I'm glad if it came across, but I also think it's built in.'

The relentlessness of the anguish, and hence the relative lack of comedy, presented in Schneider's initial reading of the play began to become apparent almost as soon as other directors had the chance to tackle the material. The various different casts working under Schneider apparently remained fairly consistent in realising his interpretation: 'taking individual differences into account', Norman Nadel commented fifteen months into the Broadway run (with

Mercedes McCambridge having taken over from Uta Hagen), 'Schneider has maintained the same balance of values among the four, the same arrangement and impact of dramatic accents' (Nadel 1964). The following year, however, when Edward Parone gained permission to direct a stock production in Paramus, New Jersey, the New York critics who made the trip across the Hudson found a refreshing variation on the original. Though much of the emotional force of the Broadway version had been lost, Jerry Tallmer commented in the *New York Post*, 'the show emerges as more a comedy than when we first saw it. I do not think this injurious: the humor and specifically the intellectual humor – in fact the intellect – of *Virginia Woolf* has been scanted among all the wooly praise' (Tallmer 1965).

When Albee himself came to direct the play in 1976, the play's wit was given fresh emphasis thanks to his focus on the rhythmic dynamics of the text. In the judgement of *New York* critic Alan Rich, Albee's version was 'superior to my recollection of Alan Schneider's original work' because of 'a tension in his timing, a tautness in his line of action' which operated to underscore the play's 'harsh, hollow laughter' (Rich 1976). The general critical consensus was that the sharper pacing of this production made the play both much funnier and less of an ordeal, since the play's overall running time was cut drastically (from the three-and-a-half hours of the 1962 version to just over three hours). For *The Soho Weekly News'* Robb Baker, though, the key point was that, 'for the first time . . . George and Martha and their two late-night guests are real people that we can laugh with and at. They're human beings, not mere walking personifications of Absolute Venom and Hatefulness', as a result of which 'we begin to care about them' (Baker 1976). Thus the play's 'fierce compassion', which the *New York Times* had been almost alone in noticing in Schneider's production (Taubman 1962), became more generally apparent, as the impulse to look down on the characters with pity or disgust was diminished.

The key to Albee's approach seems to have been his pursuit of a kind of measured restraint in the playing, an avoidance of the obvious temptations to indulge in emotional fireworks, which allowed the language itself to come to the foreground. Conversely though, the play has also successfully been realised by being pushed even beyond the pitch achieved by Hagen and Hill, emphasising instead a sense of a very physical warfare. When the Yugoslav company Atelje 212 brought their version of *Virginia Woolf* to New York's Lincoln Center in 1968, the perspective of several critics was summarised by the *Morning Telegraph*'s Whitney Bolton, who felt that this production 'penetrated far more deeply into Albee's play than Alan Schneider ever did', because Schneider 'held it within rigid limits when, in truth, it arrived at scenes requiring more candid and even more violent expression.' Mira Trailovic, however, directed 'all four players [in] moments of decisive emotionalism', and created 'a scene in which George, in a moment of uncontrollable rage, beats Martha with his fists', which gives him 'more substance than he had originally, more shape as a fallible man with limits to his toleration and patience' (Bolton 1968). For Dan Sullivan of the *New York Times*, the pouring out of such violent emotion allowed for more of a sense of *exorcism* by the play's conclusion, and thus, paradoxically, 'there are distinct intimations that things will be much better' (Sullivan 1968).

Clearly then, there is a wide range of possibilities for productions of *Virginia Woolf* to explore. As newspaper reviews like to make clear, each new rendition suggests somewhat different emphases on the play's basic components of love, hate, violence, restraint, comedy, tragedy, despair and hope. Talking in generalities about productions on the basis of such reviews, however, is of limited critical value, not only because of the necessarily impressionistic brevity of the form, but because different reviewers' critical standards are bound to vary. For example, when Mercedes McCambridge took over from Uta Hagen in the Broadway production in January 1964, she was praised by Norman Nadel for the understated restraint of her portrayal of the part; her 'deadly effective way of holding herself in check for a few seconds before triggering her anger' (Nadel 1964). In Doric Wilson's view, however, this restraint suggested a tentative lack of commitment: 'Mercy, who was a friend, played the whole show on tippy-toe. Later at Richard Barr's I got both loud laughs and cold stares when I said it was "a night at the ballet."' Given the limitations of relying on secondhand reports, I propose to devote the remainder of this chapter to a comparative analysis of five different performances of *Virginia Woolf* which exist in recorded formats and so can be compared and contrasted in retrospect. These are, in chronological order: the 1963 CBS audio recording of the original Broadway cast; the 1966 Warner Brothers film adaptation; the BBC radio version, produced by Glynne Dearman and first broadcast on 2 July 1974; an audio recording of the 1981 National Theatre production, taped in performance on 28 October (two months after the 27 August opening); and a video recording of the 1996 Almeida Theatre production, taped in performance on 22 October (a month after the 25 September opening). This last I have used to supplement my own memories of seeing Howard Davies' production in the West End at the Aldwych Theatre that November.

A number of caveats should be noted before proceeding with this analysis. We are not comparing like with like here: only the radio and film versions can still be appreciated in the medium for which they were made, while only the performances in the film and video can be seen as well as heard. The live theatre recordings, conversely, have the distinct advantage of audiences responding very audibly to the play's humour, but of course such recordings do not allow for 'retakes', meaning that any errors made once and once only in that performance are preserved forever.

Even more problematic is the CBS recording of Schneider's original production, in which a performance designed for the stage and played for months in front of capacity audiences is reproduced in the curiously sterile environment of a sound studio. There is something hollow-sounding about the whole recording, not least because the actors are still (naturally enough) projecting their voices as if in a large theatre, despite the locality of the microphones. The cast reportedly hated the recording process, which was carried out on a mock-up of the stage set which was too shallow to allow them to act as normal, and with Albee himself watching to see that they stayed word perfect with his script. After months of performances, minor variations in phrasing had inevitably crept into their performances, but the author was unwilling to have these appear on record. According to George Grizzard, Albee even required Hill to deliver one speech direct from the script, 'which was very damaging to his performance' (McNally 1982: 21). All this said, however, Schneider believes not only that the actors coped well with the awkward conditions, but that the tensions lent an added edge to their performances, resulting in 'the most spontaneous and exciting recording of a stage play I have ever heard' (Schneider 1986: 331). Critic John Gassner believed that 'the recording does not fail to project the soul and substance of the play' – or rather, of the stage performance of the play with which he was already familiar (Gassner 1963: 39).

If these recordings must be taken as approximate documentations rather than as definitive representations of the productions in question, the great advantage of them – nevertheless – is that the general flow and dynamic of those performances is captured effectively. The impressions created by these recordings tally in important ways with written critiques, and by cross-referencing recordings and reviews it is possible to present fairly accurate analyses of the relative merits of the performances in question – analyses which also suggest more general critical points about the play in production. None of what follows, however, should be seen as taking away from the fact that all five of these performances are of a very high quality. The distinctions I will be making are intended to explicate differing degrees of success in presenting Albee's play, as opposed to degrees of failure.

BALANCING THE PERFORMANCE

The 1963 recording of Schneider's original cast is particularly interesting in bearing out critical reports of that production being played at a fairly constant pitch of aggressive intensity. From the very first moment, in which Hagen bursts into earshot with a deep, booming belly-laugh, prior to an explosive delivery of 'Je*sus* H. Christ', the tone of all-out attack on Albee's script is established. 'Uta entered the stage like a runaway locomotive and took your breath away much as a blow to the gut will', Doric Wilson remembers of Hagen on stage. Yet despite some sense of ebb and flow in the performance there is an increasing impression, in listening to the recording, of a lack of much variation in pace or tone over the course of the play. The protagonists seem intent on tearing into each other from start to finish, which results in a certain sense of overall shapelessness – at least for listeners to the record who have not the benefit of seeing the staging. That impression is strongly reinforced when one compares the CBS recording with the BBC radio production, which features Elaine Stritch (one of Hagen's matinee stand-ins on Broadway in 1963) and Ray McAnally (who took over from Hill in London in 1964). This version begins more quietly, with a clear sense of the two protagonists arriving home late and tired, and casually entertaining each other with banter and playful abuse, until the arrival of their 'guests' sparks the first real moment of head-on conflict, over whether or not Martha has the right to mention 'the kid'. From this point on, there is a steadily mounting sense of tension as Stritch and McAnally try to score points off each other in front of their guests. One can actually locate specific moments at which the stakes are raised further in a spiralling tit-for-tat war of attrition: George refuses, frankly but firmly, to light Martha's cigarette as if in retaliation for her mouthing off too much; Martha responds by starting in on 'body talk', discussing Nick's body and George's paunch in a deliberate exploitation of her husband's insecurities; George exits and returns with the gun which he aims at Martha. All of this is of course apparent in the text, but the step by step intensification is far more apparent in Stritch and McAnally's interpretation because they start more quietly and easily. The mounting tension then reaches an audible peak in Act II: 'SNAP! It went snap,' Stritch declares with chilling force: 'There is no moment . . . there is no moment any more when we could . . . come together' (95). The couple really have pushed something beyond breaking-point this time; 'total war' has been precipitated and will inevitably result in the climax of the baby's 'murder' by George in Act III. That gesture is itself clearly played by McAnally as if it is his last trump card, the only act George can think of which would outdo Martha's attempts to cuckold him.

Broadly speaking, the intensification approach adopted by Stritch and McAnally creates a greater sense of crisis in George and Martha's relationship precisely because, having started as if their initial banter could have taken place at any time over the last fifteen or twenty years, their battle becomes steadily darker and more menacing, steamrolling towards a life-changing climax. By contrast, Hagen and Hill's relentless flaying of each other results, paradoxically, in the impression that this has all happened any number of times before; perhaps it is a routine they lay on for unsuspecting guests. Thus the emotional stakes do not seem quite as high, even though the pitch of the battle is more relentless. Rather, it seems that George and Martha's only means of communication is through their wilful cruelty to each other – a circumstance which has apparently existed for years and could continue to do so indefinitely. Of all the recordings under consideration here, Hagen and Hill's rendition suggests the most genuinely sadomasochistic version of George and Martha's relationship. There can be little doubt that the shock value of the play in 1962 was added to considerably by these brilliantly theatrical but peculiarly heartless performances, which fully emphasised the viciousness of Albee's script, but little of the underlying compassion. One wonders whether, with a different cast and director, a greater warmth between George and Martha might have been more apparent from the outset, and whether, consequently, the play's premiere might have been less controversial.

Certainly the initial critical impression that *Virginia Woolf* is primarily about Martha seems to have resulted largely from the fact that it is Hagen but not Hill who displays substantial emotional development through the course of the performance. On record, she grows increasingly distraught, offering – in particular – a vividly tear-stricken reading of Martha's speech at the opening of the third act, and a devastated, howling response to George's 'exorcism' of the child. Hill, by contrast, maintains much the same tone of cynical, stiff-upper-lip bitterness throughout, giving very little emotionally and finally finding a way to get past Martha's defences. This contrasts sharply with the 1966 film version, in which almost the opposite happens. As in the BBC version, the general tone of the performance is initially quieter and more affectionate than in the Broadway original, but Nichols places great emphasis on comic business and 'patter' as Elizabeth Taylor's hyperactive Martha follows Richard Burton's George about the house, pestering him with conversation he does not want to engage in. Taylor's is a competent and dynamic performance, but as the film progresses she suggests little variation in her general ballbreaker-with-a-heart-of-gold approach. Burton, however, starts off tired, bored and ready to sleep (lying down on his bed and then literally being bounced on by Taylor in her attempt to get a response out of him), but then gradually tunes into the situation presented by the arrival of the unexpected guests, and begins assembling data for deployment on the offensive. One can almost see Burton's mind clicking into gear and starting to hunt for weak spots in the other characters, especially during his head-to-head confrontations with George Segal's Nick. By the time the third-act climax is reached, his intellectual and emotional control of the situation is total. 'In the move from stage to screen,' Edith Oliver commented in *New York*, 'Martha's play has become George's movie' (Oliver 1966).

That switch of emphasis is still more apparent in the recording of the 1981 National Theatre production, which elevates to almost dialectical clarity the distinction suggested by the film between George as a man of wit and intelligence and Martha as a woman of passionate emotional outbursts. Indeed one is tempted to stereotype further and suggest a contrast between a very 'British' male type (dry, understated) and a very 'American' female type (loud, brash). Paul Eddington's George, unlike Richard Burton's, at least makes some attempt at an American accent, but it has a distinct tendency to slip when he gets agitated. Yet this flaw, which was also noted in several reviews of the production, is more than compensated for by Eddington's exquisite comic timing. His is easily the funniest reading of George among the five examples being considered, and for all the vacillating weakness which Eddington also lends to the part, the degree of command over the audience and the other characters which his wit grants him makes him the undisputed centre of the performance. Margaret Tyzack, the late replacement for Joan Plowright, attempts to compete with Eddington via sheer emotional force, but she is no Uta Hagen. Though she was widely applauded by critics when the National's production opened in late August 1981, the performance taped in late October is distinguished primarily by the rather wearying monotone of her angry yelling. If, as Milton Shulman wrote in the *Evening Standard*, there was initially 'something very English and very controlled about her characterisation that ran counter to the role of a brawling, frustrated American woman', she seems eventually to have turned into a crude caricature of that Americanness (*LTR* 1981: 440). Yet this was not, perhaps, solely her own fault. According to director Nancy Meckler, it was Eddington whose performance changed most noticeably over time, as he began to treat the role of George as a kind of essay in comedic understatement: 'the thing he would do that I found astonishing is that, as the run would go on, he would set himself a target of doing less and less, just to see how little you could do and still play the role, still have impact'. Judging by the available recording, it seems that Tyzack felt she had to respond by doing more and more, almost screaming her lines in a vain attempt to counter-balance Eddington's understatement with overstatement. Imagine, for example, the following exchange played in this manner:

MARTHA: I swear . . . if you existed, I'd divorce you . . .

GEORGE: Well, just stay on your feet, that's all . . . These people are our guests, you know, and . . .

MARTHA: I can't even see you . . . I haven't been able to see you for years.

GEORGE: . . . if you pass out, or throw up, or something . . .

MARTHA: . . . I mean, you're a blank, a cipher . . .

GEORGE: . . . and try to keep your clothes on too. (*18*)

Played as a straight contrast of battering, frustrated aggression against cool, dry, perfectly timed irony, such passages result in Tyzack simply sounding pathetic and boorish. The Eddington–Tyzack performance indicates with crystal clarity the fact that *individual* choices made by actors in these roles will greatly affect the *overall* dynamic of what is fundamentally a reciprocal relationship between George and Martha. The need for detailed communication between the lead actors, so as to establish a balance between their performances, is clearly apparent through its absence in this performance. This was also the case with the 1987 Young Vic production, which Patrick Stewart regarded as such a profound personal experience, but which drove Billie Whitelaw close to nervous collapse. The reviews unanimously stress the dynamism and intensity of Stewart's performance as the key to the production, much as Eddington's comic skill was praised six years previously: in both cases, it seems, their partners were pushed into the rather thankless position of having to respond to individually oriented star turns. Perhaps the critics' emphasis on the centrality of Uta Hagen's performance in 1962 is indicative of a similar failure of communication between the leads. Given the two-way dynamic inherent in their roles, Hagen's detailed pre-rehearsal mapping out of her approach to Martha probably left Hill with little choice but to try to reciprocate the venom she was hurling at him.

By contrast, all accounts of Albee's 1976 Broadway revival indicate that the personal bond between Colleen Dewhurst and Ben Gazzara was of fundamental importance in their creation of an evenly balanced fight. Similarly, as has been noted, the great strength of the Elaine Stritch–Ray McAnally recording is the steady building of their to-and-fro, tit-for-tat conflict, which could only have been created through carefully reciprocal work in rehearsal. Much the same is also true of Diana Rigg and David Suchet in the 1996 Almeida production, so carefully directed by Howard Davies to emphasise the fluctuating power relationships among all the characters. The reasoning behind Albee's own, repeated insistence on the importance of achieving a balanced conflict is made strikingly apparent in these versions because, hardly surprisingly, the dramatic tension and suspense generated by the central confrontation is considerably greater than in those performances where one or other partner seems clearly to have the upper hand, in terms either of personal power or audience sympathy. There are some marked differences between the BBC and Almeida recordings which I will address later, but what these performances have in common, most significantly, is an *avoidance* of the gender-stereotyped dialectic between over-emotional female and over-rational, calculating male, which all the other examples here stumble into to one degree or another.

As Albee himself observes, 'Martha's always intuitive and instinctual, and George is always more controlled and intellectual. Everybody plays it that way. You have to. That's the way it's written.' Yet this broad distinction becomes problematic when it is taken too far, by creating an impression that the protagonists cannot function or even communicate on even terms. To compete in the same league with George, both Stritch and Rigg display a degree of intellectual cunning unmatched by Hagen, Tyzack, or Taylor (who is further handicapped by the cutting of many of Martha's more obviously 'clever' lines from the screenplay). Conversely, the most effective portrayals of George are arguably those which most clearly demonstrate the character's underlying emotional vulnerability. The suggestion of a weak underbelly helps to explain why George is sufficiently threatened by Martha to descend to the level of intellectual cruelty which he exercises in Acts II and III. There is something of this instability in Eddington's performance, but McAnally and Suchet both suggest a more dangerous volatility. One simple exchange in Act II helps illustrate this point:

> GEORGE [*pensively*]: I used to drink brandy.
> MARTHA [*privately*]: You used to drink bergin, too.
> GEORGE [*sharp*]: Shut up, Martha!
> MARTHA [*her hand over her mouth in a little girl gesture*]: Oooooops.
> NICK [*something having clicked, vaguely*]: Hm?
> GEORGE [*burying it*]: Nothing . . . Nothing. (76–7)

McAnally, in particular, plays the 'Shut up' with a sharpness which suddenly seems out of place in the general desultory tone of the conversation; he is stung by her mention of 'bergin' and erupts before he can control himself. It is this slip which prompts Martha's mocking 'Oooooops': she knows she has caught him out and momentarily shattered the studied cool. This moment only works, though, if controlled understatement has indeed been George's general tone prior to this moment. If, as with Hill, the general impression is of a (to borrow Martha's phrase) 'portrait of a man drowning', then George never really seems to be in control of the situation, and so Martha's (Hagen's) mockery of his outburst seems unnecessarily cruel. Stritch, however, plays the 'Oooooops' with a degree of subtly pointed irony which emphasises both McAnally's slip and her skill in producing it. In their tit-for-tat battle, an almost exact reversal of the same moment is then produced shortly afterward, as they attempt to be heard over Beethoven's Seventh Symphony:

> MARTHA: Cut it out, George!
> GEORGE [*pretending not to hear*]: What, Martha? What?
> MARTHA [*as GEORGE turns up the volume*]: CUT IT OUT, GEORGE!
> GEORGE: WHAT?
> MARTHA [*gets up, moves quickly, threateningly, to GEORGE*]: All right, you son of a bitch. . . .
> GEORGE [*record off, at once. Quietly*]: What did you say, love?

MARTHA: You son of a . . .
HONEY [*in an arrested posture*] You stopped! Why did you stop? (*79*)

The obvious way to play Martha's lines here is to repeat 'You son of a . . .' with approximately the same force as before, only to be interrupted before completing the phrase (Hagen actually does complete it in the CBS recording). Stritch's Martha, however, allows her line to tail off into silence, smart enough to realise that she has now been caught out, in turn, over-reacting to a deliberate provocation. Here, George racks up a point to cancel out the one she scored moments earlier. He then switches gear by making eyes at Honey ('Hi, sexy'), with the result that Martha one-ups him by initiating dancing with Nick. Throughout, there is a sense of a screw twisting tighter with each new variation on the conflict, but that only works because the protagonists are so evenly matched in both intelligence and emotional ruthlessness. Similarly, as several critics commented of the 1996 Almeida version, 'Rigg and Suchet are splendid at communicating the depths of Martha and George's vulnerable dependence upon one another'; 'they are equal partners in . . . that special kind of cruelty of which only the vulnerable are capable. No other production I have seen has brought this out quite so clearly' (*LTR* 1996: 1232, 1229).

MARTHA

The preceding discussion should not be taken as invalidating the usual tendency, among critics and performers alike, to see Martha as a raw-edged, highly emotional character. That emotionalism should not be allowed to obscure her other qualities, but there is no question that the role is a peculiarly intense one. By all accounts, however, the part is not as physically tiring to play as one might expect: 'this play stimulates you,' comments Nancy Kelly, 'it fills you with vitality' (Smith 1964). 'This is an exhilarating thing,' Hagen's London

replacement Constance Cummings concurs: 'It's like having a marvellous day of exercise. You're not tired, you're refreshed' (Jones
1974: 10). Yet the psychic effect of having to internalise and project
Martha's pain and fury should not be underestimated. Elizabeth
Taylor, who did not even have to play the part on stage, claims that
'while I was playing *Virginia Woolf,* for something like a month, I was
schizophrenic. I would go home and bawl and curse because I was
trying to find Martha. I must have been a demon around the house'
(Jones 1974: 10). Burton confirms that she began living the role to an
extent she did with no other part before or after this, and could be
abusive and irritable in social situations. Nor should this be dismissed
as misguided over-indulgence in method acting on Taylor's part.
Elaine Stritch is among others who have had similar experiences: 'It
takes over my life too much, that part. I try not to let it affect me,
after the curtain goes down, but it does. Your language gets outrageous, you spill ash on the rug, you use four letter words' (Jones
1974: 11).

Perhaps the greatest strength of Uta Hagen's performance as
Martha was her ability to make the character's passionately extrovert
behaviour seem not only plausible but *lived.* Listening to the sound
recording of her playing the part, one is still struck by the richness of
her emotional engagement, carried along by an extraordinary vocal
range (from deep, rumbling rasps of amusement to high-pitched disbelief) and her ability to lend strange poignancy to the most seemingly trivial of lines. There can be no doubt that her rigorous
preparation for the role paid rich dividends: well before the beginning of rehearsals, she had worked through every moment of the
script, applying such key Stanislavskian precepts as 'given circumstances' and 'emotional memory' in order to find appropriate psychological identification points for the character's every turn. Yet Hagen's
insistence on such studied emotionalism – 'I have to fight continually
for subjectivity' (Tallmer 1963) – seems not to have allowed for much
critical questioning of her own assumptions about the character. She
seems to have decided early on to view Martha as a character whose

primary characteristic is the display of deeply unpleasant behaviour, and she prioritised finding ways for her to exhibit such unpleasantness 'truthfully'. 'The difficulty to me as an actress is to find an identification with each psychological move so that it's me up there', and her approach to Martha was thus built on the observation that

> I don't know anybody with the most negative and vicious behavior who considers him or herself to be vicious or evil or, in the case of Martha, pardon the expression, ballbreaking. We behave badly, but we justify it when we feel that something has been done to *us*. I found Martha to be a damaged woman who was damaging back. I had no trouble justifying her or worrying whether she was evil.   (*McNally 1982: 13–14*)

Given this starting-point, it is hardly surprising that, for all the emotional texture which Hagen brought to the part, most audiences and critics of the premiere production saw Martha as a vicious ball-breaker. If, for many, 'Hill and Miss Hagen were a force of evil the instant you met them', this seems at least in part to be because Hagen, for one, was not concerned to counteract that impression, only to fill in the psychological explanation behind it (Nadel 1964). Contrast this with, for example, Elizabeth Taylor's emphasis on the need 'to project a hurtable woman underneath all that sluttish, bawdy behavior. A couple of times, my heart breaks for George and Martha. Way down under that morass of fears and complexities is a deep, close-knit intimacy, a dependency' (Thompson 1965). Certainly, while Taylor does her fair share of yelling and jabbing, she projects much more vulnerability than does Hagen in the recorded performance, and takes every opportunity to suggest a warmer subtext to the character. Her response to George's jibe of 'Martha's a romantic at heart', for example, is given an unexpectedly pointed tone of quiet seriousness: 'That I am.' If anything, however, this Martha is *too* vulnerable, and a little too dependent on George, especially in the closing moments when – like a lost child – she appears to embrace his assertion that the destruction of their imaginary son was 'necessary' for them to go on together.

If Hagen remained the definitive Martha for many, it was thanks primarily to the tour de force virtuosity of her performance. Her sheer physical presence was repeatedly highlighted by reviewers. 'Miss Hagen [stalks] her victims like a savage child clubbing at someone else's heels', commented Walter Kerr: '[She] lifts her upper lip as if anyone were free to kiss it, while reserving her lower lip and teeth for a hiss at husband Arthur Hill' (Kerr 1962a). Such comments initiated a long tradition of the actors playing Martha being described by reviews in terms which emphasise a kind of grotesque, even bestial physicality. Eileen Herlie's 1970 performance in Chicago, for example, prompted descriptions of her 'laughing noiselessly through the red slash of her mouth, slithering across a couch as she hisses out her loathing' (Christiansen), and 'bray[ing] like a bull moose' (Syse). In 1981, Margaret Tyzack was even bizarrely described by *The Spectator* as displaying 'teeth gleaming like a Cadillac' (*LTR* 1981: 440). If such comments suggest a degree of underlying, unquestioned sexism – an insistence on seeing Martha more as a repellently unfeminine body than as possessor of a cutting mind – they also indicate something of the established expectations that many now bring to the play, expectations shaped in large part by the astonishing force of Hagen's performance.

Nevertheless, those few critics who made the effort to see and report on Hagen's various stand-ins and successors in Schneider's original production quickly began to see that there were other possibilities in the role. As the first matinee Martha, Kate Reid (a former student of Hagen's) was received unfavourably by critics whose reviews of Hagen's version were barely dry: 'Miss Reid seems a fishwife with the personality of a witch . . . Miss Hagen's is a sharper, more ingenious evil' (Nadel 1962). Yet Albee himself remembers Reid's as a 'marvellous' performance, distinguished by its subtlety, and by the time that the 1963 national tour kicked off in Boston, Nancy Kelly was being appreciated by more than one critic for similar reasons: '[she] is somewhat softer, somewhat more contained than Miss Hagen, who played it with animal ferocity. Miss Kelly, however, is just as real and terrifying as Miss Hagen, but she has a tendency, I think, to make Martha a shade more sympathetic' (Kelly 1963). Looking back in his memoirs, Alan Schneider agreed that, while 'no-one ever matched Uta's virtuosity and power, Kate got more humor, perhaps, and more humanity in to the first act; and Nancy wrenched a few more tears from the third' (Schneider 1986: 330). Doric Wilson, who, as a friend and assistant to Richard Barr, saw all the various cast combinations in the original Broadway production, offers a more controversial perspective on the situation by asserting that,

> although it was sacrilege to say it at the time, Uta in fact wasn't that good as Martha, because she was so powerful she took over the stage. It's a four character play, and with other actors you saw it as an ensemble piece, even with Mercy McCambridge, but with Uta on stage it was three characters and a runaway locomotive. That curtain opened and Uta Hagen hit the stage like a 747 with no landing brakes. And three and a half hours later you went out the back of the theatre and you had been *done*. . . . The great Martha was in fact Elaine Stritch. She was definitive, as far as I'm concerned.

Wilson's reasons for this last point relate, particularly, to Stritch's approach to the final act – an issue to which we shall return later. Unfortunately, Stritch's performance as a replacement for Kate Reid in the matinee cast in 1963 went unreviewed in the press. Yet it is interesting that Albee himself, when I interviewed him for this book, praised Stritch's reading of the part in terms which implicitly stressed her avoidance of mimicking Hagen's approach: 'Stritch, as you know, can be big and bawdy, but the interesting thing [about her Martha] was that she played a very, very small performance. It was very good: she didn't go overboard, she was very subtle.'

When Albee directed Colleen Dewhurst in the part in 1976, they aimed for something similar. Predictably enough, Dewhurst's physicality was the first thing commented on by several of the critics: as Albee wryly notes, 'she *was* the earth mother'. In the *New York Times*,

Clive Barnes described her performance in terms that suggest a conflation of previous descriptions of Hagen and Taylor: 'With a raspy, gin-flaked voice and subterranean chuckles, Miss Dewhurst is like a little girl lost in middle-aged baby fat', but also oozes sexuality via 'gleaming eyes, fierce nostrils, the very stance of her body in its bulging jeans' (Barnes 1976). Nevertheless, the critics were most impressed by the 'subtle hints of terrible inner inadequacy' which Dewhurst brought to the role. 'She's a strong, somewhat (but not overly) abrasive woman who spends most of her time trying to hold on to what she has', commented the *Soho Weekly News*.

> Dewhurst's Martha is far less flashy than Uta Hagen's or Elizabeth Taylor's. . . . She's not really out to destroy, [she] is not particularly dislikeable, and because she doesn't become a larger-than-life Bitch Goddess . . . the interpretation fits in with the overall directorial concept that Albee seems to be aiming for: humanizing the play so that people see its ideas and nuances, not just its verbal/emotional pyrotechnics. (*Baker 1976*)

Dewhurst herself commented that Albee had 'helped me track down the character of Martha, helped me make her more human – not just neurotic, and not stupid' (Stern 1976: 5). Though no recording survives of this interpretation, it seems to me that the tapes of Elaine Stritch and Diana Rigg preserve performances with a similar combination of intelligence and humanity alongside the pain and anger.

Of these two, Stritch's is by far the more understated reading of the part: her 1974 radio rendition seems to have preserved the subtlety which Albee so appreciated in her performances eleven years earlier. What is most striking, in comparing her recording directly with Hagen's, is the wry dryness of her whole approach. Where Hagen misses no opportunity to cut Hill down with mockery, Stritch's loudest laughs tend to be reserved for McAnally's jibes at *her*, as if she knows this is all a game between them at the guests' expense. She draws particular amusement, for example, from his suggestion that the painting on their wall is a pictorial representation of the order of her mind, and even applauds George after his 'I will not give up Berlin' speech – apparently in admiration for the virtuosity of his improvisation. Except in the most inflamed moments, Stritch treats proceedings with a knowingness and wit which conjures an unnerving sense of her toying with her listeners, so that nothing she says can necessarily be taken at face value. Her story about her brief first marriage, told to Nick late in the first act, is especially telling in this regard. Uta Hagen's reading of this passage makes it sound as if the events Martha describes at 'Miss Muff's Academy for Young Ladies', where she lost her virginity to the gardener's boy, are based on real memories, even if the names have been changed for effect: there is an almost wistful quality of the remembrance of things past. No doubt this is an effect of Hagen's Stanislavsky-based approach of hunting for 'events and possible substitutions from her own life which would imaginatively fuse her own life with the imagined world of the play' (Spector 1990: 185). By contrast, Stritch's version of the Miss Muff speech is far more ambiguous, and sounds almost as if she is making it up as she goes. For example, with the line 'my sophomore year at Miss Muff's Academy for Young Ladies . . . college' (52), Stritch's insertion of the word 'college' sounds more like a retroactive renaming of the institution (college sounding better than academy?) than the explicatory note it is for Hagen. The offhand line about the college being 'a kind of junior Lady Chatterley arrangement' then seems (logically enough) to spark the idea of her seducer being a gardener. Stritch's bone-dry delivery of 'He mowed the lawn at Miss Muff's, sitting up there, all naked, on a big power mower, mowing away' suggests rolling, playful inventiveness more than embroidered 'truth'. By the time she comes to the part about her being 'revirginized' after the marriage's annulment, Stritch is audibly snickering to herself. The whole speech seems more geared toward an attempt to tell Nick a dirty story – thereby initiating 'blue games for the guests' and getting one up on George – than toward revealing anything reliable about Martha's past.

Diana Rigg's Martha, in line with Howard Davies' production in general, suggests a similarly self-conscious use of language games. From the very outset of the performance, she and Suchet knock lines back and forth between each other almost as if they are a double act improvising new material. Indeed, the opening is noticeably more pacy and upbeat than Stritch and McAnally's weary, mutual boredom. Rigg lacks Stritch's seemingly bottomless sense of irony, but substitutes this with a physical and emotional forcefulness reminiscent of Uta Hagen: 'If there was a part Diana Rigg was born to play, it's this one', wrote Georgina Brown in the *Mail on Sunday*. 'The Amazonian build (all the better for ballbreaking), the jutting jaw (all the better for snapping with), the irrepressible sexiness . . . the smoked voice . . . add up to a huge performance' (*LTR* 1996: 1228). In an interesting reversal of the critical preferences of 1962, however, the size and force of Rigg's performance became an obstacle that one or two reviewers could not see past, and Albee himself seems to have felt similarly: 'I'm not sure that she gave me a Martha who was enjoying everything she did as much as she might have. A little too much surface angst there, perhaps.'

My own perspective, however, is that Rigg's performance represented an intriguing fusion of the kind of towering physical presence which Hagen had apparently brought to the role, and the underlying shrewdness and complexity suggested by Stritch. To quote Michael Billington's *Guardian* review, Rigg was 'much more than the conventional blowsy drunk: she presents us with a highly intelligent woman conscious of her power as the college president's daughter, yet who at the same time is haunted by self-disgust' (*LTR* 1996: 1231). Rigg's combination of power and self-awareness became most strikingly effective in moments such as her assertion, late in Act II, that George *can* stand her abuse of him:

MARTHA: YOU CAN STAND IT! YOU MARRIED ME FOR IT!!
GEORGE [*quietly*]: That's a desperately sick lie.
MARTHA: DON'T YOU KNOW IT EVEN YET?
GEORGE [*shaking his head*]: Oh . . . Martha.

MARTHA: My arm has gotten tired whipping you.
GEORGE [*stares at her in disbelief*]: You're mad.
MARTHA: For twenty-three years!
GEORGE: You're deluded . . . Martha, you're deluded.
MARTHA: IT'S NOT WHAT I'VE WANTED! (*92*)

In most of the other performances discussed here, this moment tends to sound like an outburst in which Martha is not fully aware of what she is saying. Whether or not George's 'desperately sick lie' line is played with dismissive contempt (Hill) or as if he is actually acknowledging that she has hit a nerve (Burton, most memorably), his patronising comeback then tends to reduce her to inchoate yelling. Rigg, though, seems positively titanic in those initial declarations, as if she knows exactly of what she speaks, and it is Suchet who is thrown onto the defensive. Her voice then takes on a forcefully bitter weariness, verging on tears, which invests lines like 'my arm has gotten tired whipping you' with a profound sense not only of how much she has had to swallow and put up with in this marriage, but of how disgusted at herself she is for having to be strong all the time, having to be the one who beats him into action, and having – most perversely of all – to love him. 'The key to Diana Rigg's Martha is that she understands George completely and understands why and how badly she needs him', John Peter wrote perceptively in *The Sunday Times*: 'Her restlessness and anger would be unendurable if there were not a witness, a punchbag, a guardian, a collaborator such as George to absorb them. Rigg knows that Martha loves and loathes George as you can love and loathe only someone as perversely indispensable to you as you are to them' (*LTR* 1996: 1230). Her self-recognition and resultant self-loathing are epitomised by Rigg's flailing, tormented delivery of the lines 'I'll make you sorry you made me want to marry you . . . I'll make you sorry you ever let yourself down' (104).

That last phrase is conspicuous in being omitted from Hagen's recorded performance: this may have been simply a one-off error on her part, but it also typifies the extent to which her Martha's attacks are generally turned outward rather than in on herself. She cannot concede an inch of ground to Hill when they are together, and it is only with Hagen's delivery of the speeches which open Act III (first to herself, then to Nick) that a distinct tone of self-loathing emerges, suggesting that she needs to be alone before she can confront her own inadequacies. This sequence of the play is the one in which the particular strengths of any given interpretation of Martha are showcased most succinctly, and there is no disputing the effectiveness of Hagen's performance here, as she moves through a brilliantly textured range of emotional states. From the playful, little-girl voice with which she conducts the imaginary dialogue between herself and George, through tired resignation, tearful frustration and angry railing, to sad, self-loathing laughter, Hagen presents the 'clink clink' speech (109–10) as an essay in emotional instability and desolation. That painful, self-absorbed tone then continues and grows still darker and more desperate as she describes to Nick the sick cycle of her 'would-be infidelities' with 'impotent lunkheads' (111–12).

None of the other performers discussed here brings so rich a range of feeling to these speeches as Hagen does. In the film, Taylor does not even get the chance to attempt this sequence, since most of it (including the entire opening speech) is cut. Stritch's and Rigg's more self-conscious Marthas, however, are again very interesting in this section and, unlike Hagen, both opt for a noticeable shift in tone once Nick has entered, apparently prompted by an awareness that performing pain for him is a very different thing from Martha performing pain for herself. Indeed, in Rigg's case, that notion of acting is foregrounded from the outset: she makes very clear Albee's bracketed stage direction which explains that Martha 'amuses herself with the following performance' (109), by playing the opening speech as a sadly, sardonically amusing series of imagined dialogues with George, with Daddy, and finally with herself ('Martha, you'll be a songwriter yet'). In the absence of someone else to help fill in the silence, Rigg's Martha can be seen striving to fill it for herself. With Nick's entry, she then refocuses on him, and begins to act out the pathetic scenario she describes to him, as a little show. 'Martha makes goo-goo eyes, and the lunkheads grin, and roll their beautiful, beautiful eyes back, and . . . slap over to the bar to pick up a little courage, *and* they pick up a little courage, and they bounce back over to old Martha.' As she speaks, Rigg lopes back and forth across the stage in self-disgusted, bitterly funny mimicry of behaviour she claims to have seen all too many times.

The most chilling performance of this sequence, however, is again provided by Stritch, and she achieves this by the very simplicity with which she approaches it. A basic, underlying tone of resigned, dry sarcasm is maintained throughout the opening speech, punctuated by the occasional involuntary sob or snigger. She is also clearly very drunk (a point which is not especially apparent in the other performances), her voice noticeably thicker and slower than previously. It is difficult to escape the conclusion that Stritch is here drawing directly on her own history as an alcoholic. Indeed, mid-way through the speech, her voice suddenly shifts from drunken self-pity to a more matter-of-fact tone of self-disgust, as if she is fully aware of her own attempts to delude herself. She describes with unnerving clarity how 'we both cry all the time, and then, what we do, we cry, and we take our tears, and we put 'em in the icebox' (110). Her insistent repetition of the word 'CLINK!' at the end of the speech suggests not the vacant, giggly boredom typical of other performances, but an entire life of cyclically, deliberately reaching for another glass in full self-knowledge of what she is doing. Once Nick has entered, she prefixes the 'lunkhead' speech by playing the lines 'You're all flops. I am the Earth Mother and you're all flops' with a deliberately over-acted tone of slurred drunkenness. She then cuts this out with the abrupt 'I disgust me' (111). The rest of the speech sounds like a slow, deliberate twisting of the knife of this awareness: exposing all this to Nick somehow feels, in this performance, like the ultimate in abject self-punishment.

GEORGE

Though Martha is still often regarded as the 'flash' part in *Virginia Woolf*, the role of George is, in many respects, the harder one to play, since it is both the more re-active (George's behaviour, from the outset, is determined largely by his responses to Martha's provocations) and the more verbally active (George spends considerably more time on stage and has many more lines to speak). Somehow the actor must find a way to pitch his performance so that George's gradual assumption of control over the proceedings does not come to seem out of proportion with the challenge he is reacting to. The actor must also decide whether his responses to Martha should attempt to match her in head-to-head aggression, fighting fire with fire, or whether to act as a punchbag who absorbs her blows and tries to undermine her more subtly. The *New York Times* review of the original production gives the impression that Arthur Hill went for the latter option in his battle with Uta Hagen: 'Mr. Hill gives a superbly modulated performance built on restraint as a foil to Miss Hagen's explosiveness' (Taubman 1962). Given the horror with which most critics initially regarded Martha, however, the 'restraint' described here might simply refer to George's avoidance of actually physically attacking her; his decision to destroy her psychologically. The performance of Hill's which survives on record seems more consistent with those critics who emphasised a viciousness almost as pronounced as Hagen's. Walter Kerr, for example, celebrated 'the delectable meanness with which he pretends interest in a bore' (that is, Nick), and the way 'his quick, callous, fiercely fanciful tongue is busy, without rest, stripping the skin from Miss Hagen's middle-aged back' (Kerr 1962a). There is a sneering, flailing contempt about Hill's tone on record, not only in his battles with Martha but also, particularly, during his assaults on Nick and Honey in 'Get the Guests', which gives his performance undeniable force but not, unfortunately, a great deal of subtlety or variation. Hill's apparent discomfort with the recording process needs to be considered here, as does the high praise he received from critics at the time. Yet based on the available evidence, and the comparisons which hindsight has made possible, his performance was not especially effective in bringing out the complexities of the character. There are, to be sure, some wonderful 'technical' touches, as befits an actor whom Alan Schneider describes as working out his every last piece of stage business with choreographic precision. His rhythmic refilling of drinks, for example, is often used to punctuate speeches to great effect: 'And while she was up [CLINK, the ice cube is dropped into the glass] you married her [CLUNK – the tongs are dropped back in the bucket]' (60). Yet his portrayal lacks important features of the role which subsequent actors have made far clearer.

Perhaps the most serious shortcoming of Hill's performance is that he does not give the impression of George being especially intelligent. This can, certainly, be seen as a legitimate interpretation of the circumstances: George is a 'bog' in the history department who has not proved to be the high-flyer some expected him to be. Yet that stagnation becomes all the more tragic if the play gives the impression of enormous potential having been wasted or stifled, and Albee's script provides plentiful support for this reading: George's endlessly inventive language games suggest a still-quick, restless mind which now has nothing better to do with itself than invent ways to tease and bewilder smaller wits (what Martha calls 'pigmy hunting'). Hill, however, delivers many of these speeches more or less on a monotone, as if he were a bored teacher reciting from a textbook, rather than a virtuoso improvising on the spot – as, for example, Ray McAnally suggests (for all his world-weariness, McAnally is a perfect match for Stritch in creating a sense of spontaneous inventiveness). Given the sheer size of George's speaking role, the result of Hill's comparative heavy-handedness is that, in the CBS recording, the play *does* sound unnecessarily prolix in places, just as some of the initial critics suggested. It is interesting to speculate in this respect, as in others, whether a different original cast could have saved Albee from some of the judgements initially levelled against his writing. Perhaps even the accusations of portentousness thrown at the play's supposed 'message' can be partially understood in relation to Hill's performance, since his delivery of such lines as George's quotation from Spengler's *Decline of the West* – 'And the west, encumbered with crippling alliances . . . must . . . eventually . . . fall' (104) – seem to be striving for some ominous significance. Actors like McAnally and Suchet have delivered this line with the kind of layered irony which suggests some cryptic personal joke and, more importantly, a great personal pain: George is reading aloud to try to blot out what is happening elsewhere in the house. Hill, though, does not even use the brief, 'rueful' laugh which Albee specifies as following the quote.

The lines which seem best to sum up Hill's George come from Martha, following a rambling speech of George's in Act II which Hill delivers with particular ponderousness: 'Have you ever listened to your sentences, George? Have you ever listened to the way you talk? You're so frigging . . . convoluted . . . that's what you are' (93). Hill gives the distinct impression that he has *not* listened to himself, and generally does not demonstrate much of the painful self-awareness of several subsequent Georges. Yet, in the absence of points of comparison, his performance was initially taken to represent George 'as written'. Thus, when Richard Burton offered a far sharper and more self-conscious George in the film version, more than one critic commented that he seemed *too* intelligent: 'in spite of the lines of his face and the wary or hurt or exhausted look of his eyes, it is hard to accept him as the academic second-rater he is meant to be' (Oliver 1966).

Shepperd Strudwick, who played George opposite Kate Reid, Elaine Stritch and Nancy Kelly in matinees and on tour from 1962 to 1964, was felt by those critics who compared him with Hill to offer a slightly different take on the character. A taller and somewhat more elegant-looking figure than Hill, he suggested a greater degree of sophistication in the role, and brought a greater clarity to some of his more intellectual speeches: 'Strudwick [seems to be] accenting the points of view of the restrained history professor so that Albee's argument against science becomes infinitely clearer' (Coe 1963). He was also thought to be subtler, 'deceptively mild and genteel at the start' (Nadel 1962), and in Alan Schneider's view more painfully sympathetic in the second act than Hill (Schneider 1986: 330). Nevertheless, for reviewer Norman Nadel, 'Arthur Hill is more Mephistophelean', and it was this quality that was remembered most clearly in George: as with Hagen's Martha, the abrasive unpleasantness of the portrayal was taken as definitive. As late as 1976, *New York* critic Alan Rich was suggesting that Ben Gazzara, playing George in Albee's own revival, 'lacks some of the academic cynicism that irradiated Arthur Hill's archetypal performance'.

Gazzara's performance, however, in line with the other elements of Albee's production, was tailored toward avoiding this kind of abrasiveness, opting instead for what the *Village Voice* called 'the most courageous, and at the same time the shrewdest, tactic; understatement. When he speaks, quietly, precisely, shaping his sentences, you can feel the "blood under the bridge"' (Novick 1976). The critical consensus on Gazzara's performance was that by playing George as 'a quiet man of considerable inner strength', new sense had been made of the character's situation: he is 'a loser in a way, but an urbane, witty and terribly intelligent man who has sublimated his dreams, but has not given up on life. The fact that he wins the battle of words and wits with his wife . . . now comes as no surprise. He's a strategist from the beginning, and you know that behind his mask, he's a survivor' (Baker 1976). Similar comments could also be applied to Richard Burton's George, although 'urbane' would not quite apply. 'A performance of electrifying charm', was the phrase chosen by the *Village Voice*'s Andrew Sarris, for whom 'Richard Burton reading the jokes of Edward Albee' was the film's main attraction. Burton's charm and wit, however, exists alongside a controlled intensity which suggests all sorts of repressed inner demons. Highlighted by Nichols' almost intrusive use of facial close-up, Burton's eyes seem to glint with possibilities for mischief. He too, though, is 'a loser in a way': the pain suggested here is that of a man who *knows* he should have had the resources to do so much more with his life, but somehow never overcame his own inertia. 'There is always the intimation of great power held in check in his performance', commented Edith Oliver: 'If this George is a failure, it could be only by his own choice' (Oliver 1966). The resulting, unnerving, impression is that Martha's misbehaviour – which Taylor plays as the tantrums of a spoilt, frustrated child-woman – becomes little more than the excuse George needs to offload his own self-loathing by destroying her and the guests she has invited in. It is not until much later, when George returns home on foot from the roadhouse to find Martha's and Nick's discarded clothes that the outward control really cracks, and the inner torment momentarily pours out as he weeps convulsively on the porch step. This moment, of course, does not actually appear in the play, but it stands in as an alternative to George's bitterly tearful hurling of Spengler's book against the door chimes. Burton vividly communicates a sense that George knows Martha's attempt to cuckold him is on some level his own fault, that he drove her to it with his pretence at indifference. His tight-lipped delivery of the line accusing Martha of a 'desperately sick lie', for her suggestion that he married her in a masochistic desire to be made to suffer, suggests that she has hit a very raw nerve.

Paul Eddington's performance suggests something else again – an immensely intelligent and witty man whose pain stems from an awareness that he does *not*, and never did, have the inner emotional resources necessary to have made more of himself. He shares with Hill a sense that George's situation is the consequence of a fundamental weakness of personality: unlike Burton, his failure was inevitable rather than his own fault. Yet Eddington's performance is in many ways the opposite of Hill's, absorbing Martha's abuse like a sponge and responding with a disarmingly playful-seeming use of exquisitely timed wit which hurts its targets by implication rather than by open hostility. Eddington, unlike Hill, is a natural comedian: where the latter's attempts at humour mostly manifest themselves in a tone of droll amusement at the ridiculousness of others (his early speech describing Martha's drinking history is a good example),

Eddington goes unashamedly for entertaining his audience, telling George's stories not to intimidate or belittle, but as if they were part of a stand-up comedy act. In Albee's words, 'it was a kind of boulevard performance that worked'. Contrast, for example, Eddington's and Hill's treatments of George's description of the imaginary son: 'Martha does not want to talk about it . . . him. Martha is very sorry she brought it up . . . him' (48). Hill forcefully punches in the punctuating 'him' as if it were a kind of verbal club to reinforce his control of the moment; Eddington treats it as if it were an afterthought each time, almost apologetically adding the syllables after just the right length of pause to create maximum comic impact. Likewise, George's description of Martha's father – 'Your father has tiny red eyes . . . like a white mouse. In fact, he *is* a white mouse' (51) – is blatantly abusive coming from Hill, and a genuinely funny joke coming from Eddington.

Eddington's mastery of his craft is such that he can bleed a degree of grotesque humour out of passages that no other actor under examination here has attempted to treat with anything other than total seriousness. His description of the 'bergin' boy killing his own father by inept driving – 'he swerved to avoid a porcupine, and drove straight into a large tree' (62) – emphasises the absurdity of the image even as the human horror remains apparent. On the tape recording, you can hear hastily stifled giggles in the audience – as if people are shocked at their own ability to find amusement in this. Striking as such moments are, though, Eddington perhaps loses the full ambiguity of the situation through such showmanship. The fact that his George clearly finds something amusing about the story of the car crash gives him a distance on the scenario which makes the possibility that this could be a veiled piece of autobiography seem far less likely. Similarly, when Nick queries the consistency or truth of George's Act III story of vacationing with his parents ('was this after you killed them?'), Eddington responds with a mock-ominous 'Maybe' which pokes fun so directly at his interrogator that any hint that there *might* be any truth in all this seems to be lost (118). By contrast, Burton and

McAnally both manage to conjure real mystery around these moments. Again making the most of the proximity of the camera, Burton has a tendency to cast his eyes downward, as if in pained reflection, thereby suggesting that there is actually something very personal in – for example – his story of the car crash. Could this be the story of George's own life? Of course, he has clearly not spent the last thirty years soundless in an asylum, as he says the boy in question has, but could this be a metaphoric picture of him stagnating at the college? McAnally's curious, rising yowl on the last syllable of 'he has . . . not . . . uttered . . . one . . . sound' (62) seems to be at once a hint of unspoken suffering and a kind of resigned, sick joke. He then plays the 'rather long silence' specified by Albee ('five seconds please') to full effect.

McAnally's performance does not quite boast the degree of pin-point comic accuracy which Eddington brings to the part (and radio, of course, lacks the live audience to play to, with its mounting waves of laughter). In his own way, however, he is drily hilarious – again complementing Stritch's similarly understated performance perfectly. In his first head-to-head with Nick, for example, he initially seems reluctant to have to entertain, and delivers the 'Abmaphid' speech about his own qualifications with weariness, like an old bore who has given too many lectures (as opposed to Eddington's impish mocking of academic convention). As he warms up, though, he begins to enjoy himself, jumping from idea to idea, and leaving Nick struggling to figure out the unspoken connections. His explanation to Nick that he and Martha are 'walking what's left of our wits' (27) is self-deprecating but somehow exactly appropriate. What is unsettling about both McAnally's and Eddington's performances, though, is that the apparently blithe, amusing, harmless-seeming figures they portray periodically break into viciously stinging phrases which seem to erupt almost involuntarily from beneath their intellectual defences. Eddington's private reference to Martha as 'You goddamn destructive . . .' (34) is shocking in its force precisely because he is so casual most of the time, and the absence of the word that would complete the sentence suggests that he quickly enforces self-control. Likewise, both play the speech about Martha to Nick at the start of Act II with sudden, rapid loathing and contempt: 'IT'S DISGUSTING! . . . Do you think I like having that . . . whatever it is . . . ridiculing me, tearing me down, in front of . . .' (59). The result is an unmistakable impression of intense underlying pain which belies George's laid-back veneer, but which also makes him potentially volatile and dangerous.

Martha's line to Nick in Act III perfectly captures the overall impression that Eddington, in particular, conveys: 'You think a man's got his back broken because he makes like a clown and walks bent?' (114). He is not as harmless and weak as might be assumed on first glance. Nevertheless, Eddington does lack a certain cutting edge; though his clowning can be lethal, he does not quite carry the weight necessary to inject the full measure of horror into the pivotal dramatic moments. At the conclusion of Act II, for example, he does not sound entirely convincing in his attempt to produce quiet laughter, 'mixed with crying', as Albee specifies (108). McAnally, conversely, carries this moment off with devastating effect, moving from taking a kind of malicious enjoyment in rehearsing the lines that he will use to tell Martha their son is dead, and into a kind of quietly hysterical breakdown in which tears and laughter are mixed with unnerving clarity. All the currents running under the surface of McAnally's performance seem to converge in this extraordinary moment. Hill, incidentally, neither laughs nor cries, but simply adopts a wilfully cruel matter-of-factness in his rehearsed delivery of the tragic news.

David Suchet's performance as George matches Diana Rigg's Martha as effectively as McAnally does Stritch's, and shows a similarly disturbing range of emotional registers. Suchet's George is, however, considerably 'bigger' than McAnally's – just as the Almeida performance generally is 'bigger' than the BBC Radio version (no doubt partly as a result of the differing levels of intimacy of the two media). There is a vicious force about Suchet which occasionally echoes the nastiness brought to the role by Hill (just as Rigg echoes Hagen). His first act speech to Martha, for example, building up to his refusal to light her cigarette, unmistakably underlines his absolute refusal to obey her instructions, and places her in a distinctly uncomfortable position in front of her guests: 'man can put up with only so much without he descends a rung or two on the old evolutionary ladder' (37). This is in notable contrast to the playfulness with which, say, Eddington and McAnally toy with these lines. A similar difference in force is even more apparent when Honey brings up the subject of George and Martha's son later in the act: 'When's the little bugger going to appear, hunh?' is delivered with an almost palpably threatening snarl, the 'hunh?' punched in like a fist (48).

Given this pronounced level of venom, Howard Davies' discussion of working with Suchet on his performance initially seems rather odd. Davies offers a comparison with the film version which stresses a dislike of Burton's cruelty in the George role:

> Everyone talks about this great movie, and it is a great movie, but Burton is so unpleasant in it, and so unfunny. I mean, that's a take on the character, but it seemed to me that one of George's weapons is not his masculinity, which is constantly challenged by Martha, but his wit, his intelligence and wit. He's a frustrated man who uses his wit like a lasso, he trips people up, he constantly ties them up with their own hypocrisy, or whatever. That was one of the things I was very keen on, making sure that David used his wit.

The obvious retort would be that Burton is far from 'unfunny', and that Suchet is perhaps even more devastatingly vicious. Yet Davies' explanation offers a crucial insight into the brilliance of Suchet's reading of the role by pinpointing the fact that this George is constantly undermined in his own sense of masculinity by Rigg's very strong Martha. The cruelty he displays thus springs not from an exploitation of his own control over the situation (as Burton suggests, turning his own self-loathing outward), but from a frustrated *lack* of control, as if he is desperately trying to assert his manhood. His harsher outbursts frequently occur at the points where he seems most humiliated; that is, at the points where the degree of control afforded him by his wit momentarily escapes him. He then appears still more frustrated with himself precisely because of these outbursts, his failure to keep a grip on the situation. As the performance develops, it becomes clear that his particular point of weakness is the imaginary child itself: every time mention is made of 'the little bugger' he reacts almost as if taking a blow, and frequently lashes a line back before he has taken proper control of himself.

Suchet, in short, offers a combination of wittiness and emotional vulnerability similar to that displayed by Eddington, but fuses this with an ability to hit back, with devastating effect, more akin to the performances of Hill or Burton. And though Suchet, who is often very, very funny, cannot quite match the sheer comic presence or timing of Eddington, he takes the broken-backed volatility a step further, to the point where he sometimes appears dangerously out of control. Take, for instance, the moment in Act II when George finally snaps under pressure from Martha's rhythmic recounting of how her father would not let him publish his novel. George's cries of 'DESIST! DESIST! . . . I will not be made mock of!' (82–3) sound awkwardly implausible coming from Burton, in particular, since nothing we have seen thus far suggests such weakness. Yet these lines are delivered by Suchet with the kind of pathetically enraged impotence which fully explains why he can then think of no other response than to grab her by the throat and attempt to strangle her. His poise somewhat recovered, Suchet then embarks on 'Get the Guests', in which George divulges the story of Honey's phantom pregnancy, but he is clearly not fully in control of himself, not thinking straight about the potential impact of his cruel wit on Honey. When she runs out of the room to be sick, Nick turns on him: 'You shouldn't have done that . . . you shouldn't have done that at all.' Suchet's response, 'I hate hypocrisy', comes across as a feebly irrelevant attempt to avoid the accusation, even while realising belatedly what he has just done. 'That was cruel . . . and vicious', Lloyd Owen's Nick continues, for once entirely in the right: '. . . she'll get over it', Suchet responds with a telling lack of conviction (90). Again, contrast this with Burton, who simply shrugs these suggestions off, already looking for the next point of attack, and successfully diverting the attention of the audience, who are being greatly entertained by his games. In allowing for a fuller exposure of George's 'unmanly' weaknesses, Suchet makes the character markedly less attractive, but also suggests a greater emotional complexity. 'I'm not interested in turning the role into a star performance', he told the *Daily Telegraph* as the Almeida production was opening: 'I don't care about anything but the truth of the character I'm playing' (Delingpole 1996).

NICK AND HONEY

The implicit querying of Suchet's 'getting' of the guests is indicative of the greater-than-usual emphasis which Howard Davies' production placed on the characters of Nick and Honey. The younger pair are often treated as little more than pawns in the game, but Lloyd Owen and Clare Holman brought a degree of depth and intelligence to the roles which made George and Martha's attempts both to play *to* them and *off* them seem more natural and less cynical than in most other productions. Indeed, Davies' insistence on a truly ensemble-oriented approach to the play made clear that George and Martha not only manipulate their guests, but are also utterly *dependent* on them as the focal point for their performative battle. 'I think Howard felt that George and Martha only worked *through us*', notes Clare Holman, who played Honey:

> If you just focused on Martha or on George then what you've got is kind of starry performances. But if you considered that, unless we [Honey and Nick] were there, they didn't have anything to work off, then everything had to go through us in order for them to get at each other . . . And in the process we become absolutely vital, and our responses to what they do to us become absolutely vital.

In short, Davies' production again emphasised the inherent theatricality of *Who's Afraid of Virginia Woolf?* by stressing the extent to which George and Martha need the tacit support of an audience in order to 'upstage' each other. An examination of the Almeida video recording reveals how, time and again, Davies' blocking of the actors creates clear-cut lines between those characters who are viewing and those who are viewed, with George or Martha constantly seeking to seize the initiative back from the other by rearranging those sight-lines. John Napier's set design aids this process by providing a broad, arena-like living room, in which a large, central couch and two pouffes (just downstage to the left and right of it) occupy a sunken floor area, which is surrounded by raised wings with a desk-chair and a reading chair positioned at their ends. When, for example, Martha asks Nick whether he has 'kept [his] body' (38), the pair are seated together on the couch, and are 'centre-stage' both literally and metaphorically, as she pointedly touches his knee with her hand. George and Honey are at this point standing on the two downstage wings of the stage, and George attempts to seize the initiative back by speaking *across* Martha and Nick, proposing to Honey that they 'take a walk around the garden' (a clear upping of the stakes from knee-touching). Honey, however, refuses with a giggled 'Oh, now . . .', and continues to stare awkwardly at the couple on the sofa. Realising that he cannot win like this, George exits for his gun, which will forcibly draw attention back to him. In his absence, Rigg's Martha opportunistically expands her circle of attention to take in not only Nick, but also Honey, who is drawn in off the wing to the stage-left pouffe. She is thus entirely in control of the stage and both her listeners until Suchet re-enters and puts an abrupt end to her monologue by 'shooting' her. In the aftermath of the hilarity over the gun, he then positions himself comfortably on the stage-left arm of the couch, directly in between Honey, who is seated just next to him, and Nick, who is on the stage-left pouffe. The three form a conspiratorial group staring at Martha, who is sidelined and objectified at the stage-right end of the long couch, as George describes how 'Martha paints blue circles around her things' (50).

Perhaps the single most striking use of Davies' 'theatrical' blocking strategy comes in Act II, when Martha reaches the climax of her derisive belittling of George's 'novel'. Here, Suchet finds himself caught standing downstage centre, with Martha and Nick off to either side of him and Honey behind him on the couch. All three stare and laugh at him as he protests pathetically that 'I will not be made mock of' (83). The level of humiliation created by this helpless exposure aids greatly in motivating George's subsequent, savage attacks on Martha (physically) and then on the guests themselves (verbally). Moreover, the participation of both Nick and Honey in Martha's mockery of George also makes clear that this 'audience' is far from being merely passively manipulated by the 'performers'.

One of the oldest objections to the play as a whole is, of course, that many have found it utterly implausible that Nick and Honey should stay around the house as long as they do. 'The play collapses unless it shows why they don't just get up and go', Irving Wardle commented in his *Sunday Telegraph* review of the Almeida production: 'No problem in this performance. Inside Clare Holman's fragile, giggling Honey is a voyeur turned on by violence; while Lloyd Owen marks Nick down as a career academic hanging in there to ingratiate himself with Martha, the daughter of the university President' (*LTR* 1996: 1230). Both these ideas are, of course, latent in the text itself ('VIOLENCE! VIOLENCE!', Honey cries gleefully as George attempts to strangle Martha), and Clare Holman confirms that they formed part of the thinking in rehearsals for this production: 'there's an element in it that turns them on: it's sort of fascinating, like watching a car crash or something'. Yet she points out that the couple are also held by the (somewhat more sympathetic?) desire to shore up the roles by which they recognise themselves: 'It's about holding onto that social appearance, believing that somehow they might be able to mend it, somehow they might be able to solve it . . . Yes she's been sick everywhere and yes it's all fallen apart, but if we only stay a little bit longer, maybe we could just . . .'

The complexity of the motivations which Holman identifies makes it clear that Nick and Honey, contrary to the assumptions of many, are from from being merely crudely drawn types. Nevertheless, it is also the case that, in playing these roles, there are many more 'blanks' for the actors to fill in than for those playing the leads, if only because they spend so much time listening rather than speaking. The text often gives no guidance as to Nick and Honey's reactions to what is happening, and the lines that they *are* given frequently trail off into three dots rather than offering any coherently stated response. Indeed George Grizzard, who played Nick in the original production, became so frustrated with the 'dot dot dot' lines, with the lack of clear motivations for his character, and with the near-constant mockery Nick endures from George and Martha, that 'I was really delighted to be released from the play' after only three months, in order to go and play Hamlet in Minnesota: 'I didn't mind killing six people after that' (McNally 1982: 16–17).

For all Grizzard's frustrations, though, he created a superb performance precisely because of his insistence on constantly questioning his role: 'I asked at least three times a day, "Why don't I take my wife and leave?" and Alan [Schneider] would answer, "Why doesn't Hamlet kill the King?"' (McNally 1982: 13). While Grizzard was not greatly hailed at the time, overshadowed by Hagen and Hill's fireworks, Doric Wilson is in no doubt as to the fruits borne by his interrogative approach to the part: 'he played it so brilliantly that he made the Nick absolutely right. He *was* Nick, but nobody thought he was a good actor. He was dismissed at the time because he'd had a tendency to play some creeps, like the kid in *The Zoo Story*, so people saw him playing a creep and thought "oh fine that's George Grizzard".' With hindsight, though, Grizzard's performance on the CBS recording is arguably the best structured of any in that version of the play, displaying great subtlety in his gradual intensification of the character's resentment and disorientation.

Following his first entrance, Grizzard's tone of voice initially suggests a mild degree of fawning obsequiousness toward his hosts, which clearly establishes him as a young academic with an eye on climbing the totem pole. When he is first left alone with George, however, the latter's mocking tone quickly and understandably prompts him to put up his guard: when George teases him about the way he punctuates his sentences with 'sir', Grizzard's 'no disrespect intended' is positively icy (27). On Martha's re-entrance, he begins to react to her flirting with a more openly responsive tone of voice, creating the distinct impression that, if he is to 'plough' this 'pertinent wife', it will be as much out of spite for George as ambition for himself. The revenge motive is made still clearer in Act II, when Nick responds to George's destructive 'Get the Guests' routine with a distinct tone of threat, rather than the empty blustering evident in some other performances. Grizzard's delivery of the lines 'I'll be what you say I am . . . I'll show you something come to life you'll wish you hadn't set up', suggests clearly that, if George is cuckolded, it will be his own fault for pushing Nick to it (91). Nevertheless, Nick is out of his depth in this environment, as his giggling drunkenness, and the ease with which he gave away his and Honey's secrets to George, have already made clear. His humiliation in Act III following his failure to 'get it up' thus seems pathetically inevitable, with Hagen hilariously exposing his attempts to treat her as a conquest. Yet it is hard not to feel a certain sympathy for Grizzard's portrayal: 'I didn't think Nick was a bad guy', he has commented, summing up the sense that, while his Nick is certainly not an attractive character, he does not deserve to have his pride destroyed quite this brutally: 'every time Uta or Arthur would stick a knife in they would laugh' (McNally 1982: 16).

Grizzard was replaced on Broadway by Ben Piazza, whose portrayal brought a still deeper cynicism to this 'not terribly accomplished calculator' (Albee's phrase). 'Piazza's Nick has a cruel spine to it, quite chilling in retrospect', commented Glenna Syse of the *Chicago Sun Times* when Piazza reprised the role for the Ivanhoe Theatre in 1970: 'Underneath the dumb muscle there is a calculation that is far more disturbing than anything George or Martha could conceive of.' The subtleties of Grizzard's Nick, however, are sadly missing in some subsequent renditions. In the radio version, for example, Blain Fairman's moronic, clumsily violent Nick is so inept that McAnally can run verbal rings around him during their scenes with barely any effort. Although the latter finds a kind of bored humour in realising just how easy a target he is, Fairman's performance is the weak link in this version: this Nick's bullish obtuseness certainly does not suggest a man who had finished his Masters degree by the age of nineteen. In the film version, George Segal's Nick is a more pleasant character, but lacks any real edge. Since the diversion of the narrative to the roadhouse is designed to obviate the need to explain why he and Honey stay in the house so long, Segal does not need to display much in the way of calculating ambition. As a result, though, he seems merely bland, his most memorable moment perhaps being his drunken giggling fit over his own joke about his father-in-law being a 'church mouse', which Burton observes with hilariously deadpan disdain.

Among the performances under consideration, only Lloyd Owen's Nick can compare with Grizzard's. Owen finds most of the same turning-points and suggests much the same motivations as his predecessor, but the marked differences between Arthur Hill and David Suchet also result in Owen bringing a somewhat different tone to Nick's crucial interactions with George. Where Hill was every inch the patronising superior, Suchet's more vulnerable reading of George allows for a strange kind of male bonding between the characters. It is easy to believe that Owen's tall, handsome Nick might intimidate Suchet's George, who seems at first to be attempting to shore up his own, inadequate masculinity by treating Nick as a 'buddy' figure, via backslapping bonhomie. He then abruptly attempts to lock antlers with him as soon as the women are out of the room. This switching of gears quickly begins to disorientate and anger Owen's Nick, who can deploy a viciously scathing irony all his own ('Oh sure, I'm going to be a personal screwing machine!'), and has the physical composure to follow through on his threats. 'I thought the boy was splendid', Albee himself says of Owen: 'He had a really good sexuality to him.'

I could see why Martha fancied him.' (Grizzard, conversely, was always less comfortable with the 'stud' angle of the character, and was especially self-conscious about being shorter than his stage wife, Melinda Dillon.)

The plausibility of Rigg's attraction to Owen is important in adding further to the humiliation which Suchet's George suffers as a result of their attempted adultery. Whereas, for example, in the BBC radio version, Stritch's seduction of the vacuous Fairman is clearly only a means to get at George, Rigg's liaison with Owen really is about sex, with Suchet's inadequate George forced painfully onto the sidelines. Owen actually initiates the physical contact between them, placing a hand on her belly from behind just as Rigg is fuming over Suchet ignoring her. Subsequently, they begin rubbing and kissing with a degree of candour which becomes quite uncomfortable to watch: the audience's own, voyeuristic role in the proceedings is brought sharply into focus at this point.

If Lloyd Owen created an unusually attractive, magnetic version of Nick in the Almeida production, Clare Holman's Honey was still more revelatory. On the surface, this role appears even more thankless than that of Nick – not least because Honey is given still less to work with in the text itself. She has far fewer lines than the others in the play, and spends large parts of her onstage time simply sitting around drinking, reacting to the others with varying degrees of coherence. As Holman observes, a major task for the actor is simply to figure out 'the progression of getting drunk. You see she does it very quietly, so you have to find ways of playing it physically. At what stage should she really become *that* pissed?' Even if one masters the technicalities of this process, there remains the question of how to play the character in three dimensions. For John Clum, 'Honey is a hateful caricature, a horrid case of arrested development' (186), and Holman herself admits to wondering of Albee – on first reading the role – 'ooh God, does this man like women?' Portrayals of Honey can all too easily slide into suggesting that she is simply an idiot or a 'bimbo': listening now to the recording of Melinda Dillon in the original Broadway production, for example, one is struck primarily by the almost embarrassingly artificial quality of the high, wispy, childish voice she adopts for the part, as if in an attempt to present Honey as a worse-for-alcohol version of the classic ingenue. Given the heavily gender-prescribed theatrical conventions of the time, Dillon's choices are perhaps understandable, and she was highly praised by reviewers. It might be argued, moreover, that there is *still* a good deal of audience appeal in playing up the foolishness of the role for the sake of comedy. 'Mary Maddox's simpering bunny of a wife, supping brandy and squeaking platitudes, bids fair to run away with the evening', commented the *Daily Telegraph*'s John Barber, reviewing the 1981 National Theatre production (*LTR* 1981: 439). In this case, despite Nancy Meckler's attempts to cast Honey and Nick against type, Mary Maddox's gifts as a 'very quirky performer' (Meckler), combined with the influence of Eddington's wit on the tone of the whole show, seem to have resulted in Honey being played as a freakish comic turn. As *Punch*'s Sheridan Morley cuttingly observed, 'there seems no clear textual reason for the admittedly nervy and nervous Honey to be played as mentally defective' (*LTR* 1981: 440).

Although the audio recordings of Dillon and Maddox make Honey seem disappointingly vacuous, it is perhaps unfair to assess performances of this role solely on the basis of sound, given that Honey is seen on stage so much more than she is actually heard. Certainly, the most popularly acclaimed version of the role is Sandy Dennis's portrayal in the film version, in which Honey's clear physical vulnerability and social awkwardness help generate real audience sympathy for the character. Dennis's wispy blonde hair, thin frame and baggily unflattering dress perfectly complement her facial acting, which conjures up the impression of a small animal caught hypnotised in the glare of oncoming traffic. Her initial attempts to maintain appropriate social etiquette (memorably placing an admonishing arm across Nick's body to prompt him to praise Martha's father's party) quickly disintegrate as the situation around her slips beyond her grasp and she takes refuge in the bottle – to almost uncomfortably comic effect. Although it might be argued that Dennis' portrayal suggests the female stereotype of the child-woman incapable of facing the 'real world', she brings a subtlety and depth to the character which makes Honey's behaviour entirely believable.

Interestingly, Clare Holman admits to viewing Dennis' performance while preparing for the Almeida production in 1996, acknowledging the extent to which the film version still haunts attempts to re-stage the play: 'You think, how on earth can you bring something original to a part like that? But in fact, I always find it quite useful to watch other people's performances, because you can plagiarise', she jokes: 'Steal a bit here and there and then add your own. There's an objectivity you get when you see someone else doing it.' Holman thus created a performance distinctly different from Dennis', playing up Honey's attempts at maintaining social propriety by creating an image of what she calls 'that mid-American kind of socialite-who-can-cope, in a situation she clearly can't cope with'. This was an option also explored by Pinkie Johnstone in the BBC radio version: Johnstone's delivery of lines like 'I didn't know until just a minute ago that you had a *son*' (33) are oozing with chitchat-making condescension rather than child-like enthusiasm, and her forcibly false attempts to fit in socially by laughing at what she takes to be jokes are cringe-inducing. Yet this Honey – like her husband – is fundamentally stupid, and remains little more than a stereotype. Holman, by contrast, suggests enormous complexity beneath the socialite veneer. 'There's always a two-dimensional view of every character you can play', she observes pointedly,

> but I'm always interested to find out *why* they seem that way. So if somebody says to me, Olivia [in *Twelfth Night*] is a bitch, then I'm like, well why is she a bitch? And it's the same with Honey . . . there's what she wants to be seen as, but I was just as interested in what she's trying to hide and the way she's trying to hide it . . . Because she finds herself in a kind of hellhole, where her biggest secret – about their sexual life, about her pregnancies and her destroying them – is *found out*.

Holman's performance foregrounds a vivid sense of Honey nervously attempting to keep up her respectable façade – an approach entirely in line with the emphasis of Davies' production on the characters' performativity. 'Ms. Holman's body language (the toes that turn in more and more, the finger that needlessly points to what she is talking about) is splendid semaphore of quietly hysterical social awkwardness', commented Paul Taylor in *The Independent* (*LTR* 1996: 1232). This Honey is constantly touching her skirt, as if to ensure that it is still correctly in place. Yet as she becomes more drunk, her physicality becomes looser, and when she breaks into her 'interpretive dance' in Act II, there is a clear sense of a passionate urge for release breaking out from beneath the propriety. Though the dance is usually played simply for laughs (Sandy Dennis is hilarious), Holman uses her training as a gymnast and dancer to suggest the drunk-balletic grace of someone who was once schooled in such expression and is now rediscovering the joy it brought her. When Nick then intervenes to restrain her, Holman's delivery of 'Stop that!' (79) suggests a sudden, violent resentment toward him, for this and perhaps all the other things she has had to give up to act as his wife. This outburst, moreover, is merely one part of Holman's build-up to the moment, later in Act II, when Honey turns on Nick after George has told the story of her phantom pregnancy: 'You . . . you told them . . .' (89). Here, the child-like whine of disbelief adopted in most performances of the role is replaced by a degree of distinctly adult vehemence which reduces Nick to near-speechless shame. This is not a question but an accusation, one which carries the full horror of a woman whose most personal secrets have just been publicly paraded and ridiculed. In the Almeida production, far more so than in any other under consideration here, this moment stands out as one of the most emotionally harrowing in the play.

The fresh emphasis which Holman brings to Honey's suffering also allows for a clearer focus on the subsequent revelation of her secret abortions. The trauma generated by 'Get the Guests', combined with her drunkenness, drive this Honey over the edge into disturbed, hallucinatory reflections on her rejection of children from her body: 'I don't want to be hurt. . . . PLEASE!' (105). Lying curled and cringing on the floor, her foot kicking out blindly against the blanket she is wrapped in, this is a genuinely tragic image of someone haunted by guilt over her own failures and inadequacies. Given this depiction, moreover, Honey's horror at George's plans to 'kill' his and Martha's son suddenly makes total sense: she understands as well as he does that the murder is fictitious, but makes an emotional connection to her own sense of guilt. Her attempts to stop George carrying through his plan thus read as a kind of retroactive attempt at self-redemption. When she informs him in Act III that 'I've decided that I don't remember anything . . . and you don't remember anything either' (124), Holman's emphatic tone makes crystal clear that this is a performative attempt to preempt his death narrative and send the improvisation off in a new direction. George, of course, refuses to play ball, and presses ahead despite her continued, increasingly desperate attempts at denial: 'Oh, you have a child?' (126). When she finally begins to participate in George's Latin ritual of exorcism, it is as if Holman's Honey has somehow broken through her own denials to confront and purge her sense of guilt. Here, the tearful realisation that 'I want a child!' (130) comes across as the cathartic climax of a traumatic psychological journey rather than the incidental, hysterical interjection it has seemed in other performances.

THE BIT ABOUT THE KID

Perhaps the most significant factor about Holman's portrayal is that the clarity which she brings to Honey's pain also affects one's reading of George's responses to her. At the end of Act II, with Martha and Nick having disappeared upstairs, Suchet's George is casting about for some trump card with which to hurt Martha even more than her infidelity is hurting him, and the implication is that his witnessing of Honey's abortion hallucinations provides him with precisely the spark of inspiration he needs: just kill the baby. If this is the case, though, George's 'murder' of the imaginary son in Act III is an act of wilful, calculated cruelty, of pure revenge, rather than some idealistic attempt to drive the illusions from his and Martha's marriage and face 'reality'. The assumption that George is being 'cruel to be kind' is a widely held one, not least because that is the impression conjured up by the film version, in which Burton reduces Taylor to a tearful but apparently grateful silence. Davies' production, however, allows for no such suggestion. Indeed, for Holman, Honey's attempts to stop George from pursuing this course relate largely to her horror at the sheer cruelty of what he is doing: 'she couldn't bear the awfulness, of watching him destroy someone like that'.

The political implications of Davies' production are again significant here. In the film version, Burton's brutality – which extends to the physical abuse of Honey at the end of Act II and his dragging of Martha by her hair in Act III – seems somehow 'justified' by his final act of purgation. 'Burton's performance is a marvel of disciplined compassion', commented *Newsweek*, distinguished by 'the self-contained authority of a great actor' (*Newsweek* 1966). It is as if George's responsibility as the man of the house is to restore order through the exercise of extreme sanctions against the wayward women. That impression is even more pronounced in the recording of the original production, in which Arthur Hill's heartlessly cold version of the exorcism is not so much 'cruel to be kind' as simply a necessary 'taming of the shrew', a reimposition of patriarchal control after his humiliations at the hands of the outrageous Hagen. For most critics in 1962, this seemed like the appropriate conclusion, and the 'taming of the shrew' notion was picked up on by many, not least because of Hill's particularly forceful, humourless delivery of George's third act argument with Martha over whether or not the moon is up (clearly a playful evocation on Albee's part of Petruchio's 'I say it is the moon which shines so bright'). Yet the pitilessness of Hill's destruction of Hagen's Martha helps explain why W. J. Weatherby, for one, saw the play as 'essentially misogynist' (Weatherby 1962).

10. Ray McAnally as George and Constance Cummings as Martha in the closing tableau of the 1964 London production. McAnally and Cummings replaced Hill and Hagen in the leads during the London run.

In Davies' production, by contrast, the justification for George's actions is far less clear, if there is one at all: his cruelty seems like the final, excessive response to his previous humiliations. Consequently, by the end, Rigg seems far less convinced than either Taylor or Hagen that the killing of the child was necessary: 'Did you . . . did you . . .

have to?' suggests not a trace of willing acceptance (139). The ambiguity of what the future holds for George and Martha is thus even more pronounced in this version than in most. Albee's closing tableau, in which George, seated behind and above Martha, 'puts his hand on her shoulder' as 'she puts her head back', is given a biting twist here as Rigg delivers the final line with her face turned *towards* Suchet as if in open challenge of his assumption that he has taken control of the situation. In answer to his 'Who's afraid of Virginia Woolf?', her 'I . . . am . . . George . . . I . . . am . . .' is not the usual tearful exhaustion but a calmly determined statement of fact – as if to ask 'Aren't *you*?' (And perhaps: 'Don't you know it even yet?') The negotiation of the relationship goes on, unresolved but essential to both of them.

Of the other two performances under examination here, Paul Eddington opts more for the knee-jerk revenge approach to the last act, while Ray McAnally suggests the 'cruel to be kind' angle. However, the performances of their partners alter the implications again. Eddington seems genuinely blind to the impact of what he is doing, creating a kind of twisted humour from the whole exorcism scenario, like some dangerously demented clown extending his performance a step too far. He affects the impression of real personal grief as he 'remembers' Crazy Billy arriving at the door with the telegram reporting his son's death, but only so that he can then shatter the poignancy with his wilfully sick-comic description of the boy swerving his car 'to avoid a porcupine' (135). He then uses Albee's prescribed 'tiny chuckle' to devastating effect. Even so, the listener to this recording is left with little sense of sympathy for Margaret Tyzack's overblown Martha: there is none of the horrific, tortured pain of Diana Rigg's response to Suchet (Rigg is reduced to a crouched, paralysed silence for an almost audacious length of time at the end of the exorcism scene, until Nick and Honey finally tip-toe out). If anything, Eddington seems the sadder figure here, despite his cruelty, simply because he seems to have been driven almost over the edge of his own sanity. Ray McAnally, on the other hand, maintains a cool control throughout the sequence, but unlike Burton with

Taylor, there is never any sense that he has reduced Stritch's Martha to submission. Theirs is a confrontation fought out with subtle but relentless intensity, as if McAnally is slowly, insistently prising Stritch's fingers off a whisky bottle which she grimly refuses to put down.

Each of these performances of the play's climactic stages, then, suggests distinctly different implications as to the purpose and effect of George's actions. Indeed, the continued assumption of so many commentators that the play depicts George's necessary removal of Martha's illusions so that they can face the 'reality' of their childless existence can *only* be explained by the fact that the earliest and most influential productions of the play (the Broadway original and the film version) treated the climax in this manner. I would argue, however, that these productions fundamentally *misrepresented* Albee's text, thereby generating misinterpretations that persist to the present.

Alan Schneider freely admitted that the Broadway premiere, for all its strengths, failed to deal adequately with this crucial final sequence. 'The only major area where we had a problem', he confessed in 1965, 'was the "our son" business in the third act, which I don't think we succeeded in solving. I don't blame Uta; I blame myself for not being able to help her solve it . . . Edward was blamed, but I don't think it was his fault as much as ours' (Schechner 1965: 146). Schneider attempts diplomacy here, but his mention of Hagen rather than Hill clearly implies that the fault lay with her performance. In retrospect, that suggestion seems accurate: whatever questions are raised by Hill's relentlessly unpleasant treatment of the exorcism narrative, the key mistake lay with Hagen's decision (taken independently of either Schneider or Albee, whom she accused of obfuscating the issue) that Martha has actually deluded herself into believing in the literal existence of the child. 'It was a conscious device that my husband and I had planned very early in our marriage', she explained (in character) in 1982: 'it had become reality to us, to the point where I [Uta Hagen] would have liked to see toys on the stage' (McNally 1982: 16). Consequently, Hagen played the exorcism scene with a soul-baring intensity which suggested, first, that she was actually 'remembering' the details of the boy's childhood (there is a nostalgic wistfulness about her description of 'teddy bears and transparent floating goldfish' and so forth), and, subsequently, that she was suffering the news of his actual death. The performance of all this recorded on tape is brilliant in its emotional textures, but in context actually makes very little sense: 'What is implausible about that imaginary son', Charles Marowitz commented in his *Plays and Players* review of the London production, 'is that people as blisteringly honest and sophisticated as these could resort to such a fabrication' (Marowitz 1964). Hagen's Stanislavsky-driven decision to play all of Martha's speeches about her past as if they are literally true is surely largely responsible for Marowitz's assumption that the characters are 'honest' (as opposed to incurable fabricators of language games). Yet her pursuit of this principle as far as the son results in self-contradiction, as her own work diary unwittingly indicates: 'Everything in my past – lawn mower, life with Daddy, boxing match, etc. is *true* (except for child)' (Spector 1990: 185). That bracketed rider sums up the problem: why would such a ruthlessly self-aware figure delude herself about this one, rather substantial, point? It is, however, on this choice that Hagen built her own interpretation of the play's message: 'That we carry an illusion. That we lie. That the illusion can be used not only as a crutch, but as a club. And that if that crutch, that lie, is taken away, there'll be some place to start from' (Tallmer 1963).

For various critics, the implausibilities of the original production were overcome by the film version: 'the risky Act Three', thought Dilys Powell, 'is no longer dissociated from the rest of the action; it becomes believable, passionate and moving'. Powell's explanation of her point, however, suggests that it was Burton's cruel-to-be-kind approach to the exorcism, in underlining the film's 'love story' emphasis, which made the events more palatable: 'Together Mr. Burton and Miss Taylor lend strange undertones of affection and appeal to the marital knifings' (Powell 1966). Yet there was no substantial alteration in the interpretation of Martha's responses, Taylor playing the news of the child's death with wild-eyed tearfulness. She even (perhaps unwittingly) changes the line 'you can't have him die' to 'you can't let him die', which suggests far less conscious awareness of the fact that George is performatively 'killing' the son rather than reporting a factual event. To be fair to Taylor, however, the excision of large parts of the dialogue from the exorcism sequence, including much of Martha's account of the son's infancy, made any other reading besides tearstricken grief rather difficult. The cuts were clearly made because the scene was deemed unnecessarily long if Martha's emotional responses are all that is being communicated. Yet it is in the length and detail of this exchange that the key to playing the scene lies: careful examination of the text makes clear that, far from Martha simply recounting a long-windedly nostalgic story of the child's past, she and George are both, with full self-awareness, negotiating over the details of a fictional narrative. 'Our son. You want our son? You'll have it', Martha announces defiantly, the 'it' giving away the fact that the son is an idea rather than a person. 'All right, Martha; your recitation, please', George says as he cues her in (126–7). All that is missing is 'Once upon a time'.

It was this fundamental point which Albee drew to his actors' attention when directing the 1976 Broadway revival. 'At first they *were* playing the death of a real child', Albee explained of the rehearsal process in a *New York Times* interview: 'And what we were getting was a kind of dirge-like quality . . . mourning. It was heavy and yet not really intense. After I explained the child as a kind of metaphoric game-playing, the dirge-like quality was gone. And they were playing more intensely' (Stern 1976: 5). In the same article, Colleen Dewhurst concurred that 'Edward helped me to avoid the typical woman's response to a child's death. Played his way, it's unsentimental – and just as moving.' The key to this production's success was in Albee's emphasis on the fact that the 'reality' (or otherwise) of the child is not the issue at stake; that it is the *effect* of the characters' speech acts on each other which matters. George's declaration of the child's death irrevocably changes the 'legend' of their life together,

11. Diana Rigg as Martha, with Clare Holman, Lloyd Owen and David Suchet, in the 1996 Almeida production.

and is thus every bit as devastating as news of a physical death would be. What is being destroyed for Martha is not an illusion or a delusion as such, but the very narrative structure on which her marriage to George has been built. Walter Kerr's review of Albee's production makes clear that it was the sheer emotional conviction with which Gazzara and Dewhurst played out this battle for control of a *concept* (rather than a 'truth'), which made the play make sense in a way it had not in 1962: 'When Mr. Gazzara goes to the door . . . to whip it open, welcome a messenger who isn't there, and receive – in the void filled only with the night air – a message announcing the death of the imagined son, tension is absolute. In this moment of obvious emptiness, we believe – believe that what is not happening is in some sense happening' (Kerr 1976: 7).

Unsurprisingly, Howard Davies' Almeida production also made the performativity of the final conflict very clear. Rigg and Suchet conduct their negotiation of the child's story as if playing a game of high-stakes poker, seated on the two pouffes and staring intently at one another, and across Honey, who is seated centrally on the sofa, looking between them like a spectator at a tennis match. This is visibly a two-way struggle rather than a dreamy monologue from Martha, with every tiny detail of the childhood narrative up for grabs:

> GEORGE: And for the oar?
> MARTHA [*uncertainly*] A . . . carrot?
> GEORGE: Or a swizzle stick, whatever was easier.
> MARTHA: No. A carrot. (*128*)

The combatants gradually feel each other out like this, and move on to more substantive issues. The tension between Rigg and Suchet steadily mounts as their competing versions of the child's story become increasingly dissonant – to the point where they are openly accusing each other of twisting the narrative to their own advantage rather than sticking to the established 'script':

> GEORGE: . . . [a son] who spends his summers away . . . and he does!
> . . . who spends his summers away because there isn't room for him
> in a house full of empty bottles, lies, strange men, and a harridan
> who . . .
> MARTHA: Liar!!
> GEORGE: Liar?
> MARTHA: A son who I have raised as best I can against . . . vicious odds,
> against the corruption of weakness and petty revenges . . . (*132*)

For all the frightening clarity of Rigg and Suchet's rendition, the recorded performance which arguably creates the most haunting treatment of this climactic sequence is the BBC radio version. From the moment that McAnally's George cues Stritch's Martha to begin her recitation, there is a tone of exhaustion in her voice which suggests that her words are, as Albee's stage direction states, being delivered 'by rote' (126) – a ritualistic repetition of a story told too often for the couple's own good. Then, as McAnally begins to alter details of the agreed-on story, Stritch begins to wake up from her half-conscious recitation as she realises that he is breaking their pact.

Strikingly though, she responds not with the sharp, dry wit she has displayed previously, but with an increasingly sulky tone of distrust, until, when McAnally finally announces the death of the child, she rages at him like a petulant child who has had her favourite toy taken away: 'NO! NO! YOU CANNOT DO THAT! YOU CANNOT DECIDE THAT FOR YOURSELF!' (135).

For Doric Wilson, Elaine Stritch's performance as Martha in 1963 was 'definitive' because 'she knew what the end of the play was about, probably because Elaine was an alcoholic and identified with what was going on with Martha – with what kind of delusion that is'. On tape, Stritch plays Martha not as someone who truly believes in the reality of the child, as Hagen does, but as someone who tries to pretend *to herself* that she believes it, while knowing very well that it is a fiction, an addiction which numbs her to her own inadequacies (including her inability to conceive?). Even after George has conducted his exorcism, and after the guests have left, Martha seems to be asking if her 'son' can be brought back to life, and here Stritch brilliantly captures the pathetic tragedy of the character's situation. 'I don't suppose, maybe, we could . . .' she pleads desperately, for all the world as if craving one last drink. 'No, Martha', McAnally tells her quietly but firmly. 'Yes', she says, the tone of her voice rising with an edge of defiant insistence, before dropping immediately to concede the point: 'No.' With her next line – the repetition of 'Yes. No.' – Stritch cements this sense of the double awareness of the addict. Then, after McAnally's final 'Who's afraid of Virginia Woolf?', Stritch's 'I . . . am . . . George . . . I . . . am' is a forced but firm admission of weakness. What this Martha faces now, with the removal of her 'illusion', is not some abstract 'reality', but the hard task of finding some other way to live with herself.

After all the sound and fury of the play, and indeed after all the theoretical to-ing and fro-ing of this book, we thus return to the suggestion that the fascination of *Who's Afraid of Virginia Woolf?* lies not in any simple message that can be drawn from it, nor in any reflection on the absurdity or absurdism of existence in general, but in its

simple 'naturalism'. As Stritch herself has suggested, it is the play's
confrontation of very messy but very human situations which,
finally, makes it so harrowing and so powerful:

> I found George and Martha likeable people, because they're in such
> deep trouble. There's a tremendous amount of hope in the play. I told
> Albee what I think George and Martha do when the play is over. I think
> they say, the next day: 'We won't have a drink until six in the evening.'
> That's a start.   (*Jones 1974: 11*)

SELECT CHRONOLOGY

1960

January: Edward Albee's *The Zoo Story* premieres Off-Broadway in double bill with Samuel Beckett's *Krapp's Last Tape*. Other Albee one-acts to premiere in 1960 and 1961 include *The Death of Bessie Smith, The American Dream, The Sandbox, Fam and Yam*.

1961

Summer: Albee drafts first two acts of his first 'full-length' play, provisionally titled 'The Exorcism'.

Autumn: A section of the new work is recorded for a public television series on 'Playwrights at Work'. Directed by Alan Schneider, with Shepperd Strudwick as George.

1962

Spring: Albee completes the play, now retitled *Who's Afraid of Virginia Woolf?*

13 October: premiere production opens at the Billy Rose Theatre, produced by Richard Barr and Clinton Wilder. Directed by Alan Schneider, designed by William Ritman. Starring Uta Hagen, Arthur Hill, George Grizzard and Melinda Dillon.

30 October: first matinee performance, with alternate cast (Kate Reid, Shepperd Strudwick, Bill Berger, Ava Petrides). They play two performances a week to the evening company's six.

1963

Spring: Elaine Stritch replaces Kate Reid in the matinee cast.

July: Uta Hagen and Shepperd Strudwick take vacations, replaced by Nancy Kelly and Donald Davis, respectively.

September: national road company (led by Kelly and Strudwick) opens tour at Boston's Colonial Theatre and instantly runs into censorship trouble. Tour continues through to May 1964, playing twenty-three American cities.

September: South African premiere in Port Elizabeth picketed by whites after Albee's insistence that audiences be unsegregated. Closed down for obscenity on reaching Johannesburg.

4 October: European premiere in Stockholm, directed by Ingmar Bergman as his first production for Dramaten, Sweden's national theatre.

October: German premiere, as *Wer Hat Angst vor Virginia Woolf?*, Berlin, directed by Borislav Barlog.

November: Italian premiere in Rome.

1964

January: Mercedes McCambridge and Donald Davis replace Uta Hagen and Arthur Hill in Broadway production.

February: Hagen and Hill re-open in UK premiere production at Piccadilly Theatre, London, following extensive negotiations over censorship by the Lord Chamberlain's office.

19 May: Broadway production closes after 660 performances.

July: Israeli premiere, Tel Aviv.

August: Greek premiere, Athens.

Autumn: A second American road tour begins with fresh cast but original direction/design.

November: Japanese premiere, Tokyo.

1 December: French premiere in Paris, dir. Franco Zeffirelli.

1965

March: Polish premiere, Gdansk.

August: Warner Brothers film version begins principal photography. Shot in Hollywood, and on location at Smith College, Vermont.

Directed by Mike Nichols. Produced by Ernest Lehman. Starring
Elizabeth Taylor, Richard Burton, George Segal, Sandy Dennis.

November: Paris production closes after fifty-one weeks owing to
irreconcilable dispute between its stars, Madeleine Robinson and
Raymond Jerome. Lawsuits ensue.

During 1965, the first North American stage productions outside the
Barr–Schneider–Ritman franchise are licensed (openings in New
Jersey, Los Angeles, Maine, Pennsylvania, Winnipeg, etc.).

1966

June: Warner Brothers film version released in US and UK following
extended negotiations with Motion Picture Administration of
America over the award of a Production Code Seal.

1968

July: Belgrade-based company Atelje 212 play their Serbo-Croat
production to New York audiences at Lincoln Center. Well
received by critics.

1970

September: Chicago revival at the Ivanhoe Theatre, off-Loop
(equivalent of Off-Broadway). Dir. George Keathley. Strong
ensemble cast includes Ben Piazza as Nick, reprising role he had
played in Broadway production in 1963.

November: *Variety* runs a front-page story reporting that Richard
Barr had approved Henry Fonda and Richard Burton's plans for
an all-male production. PA for Fonda and Burton confirms story,
but Richard Barr refutes it. Gender-specific casting clause is
written into all subsequent performance licences for the play.

1972

October: Spanish Theatre Repertory Company presents New York's
first Spanish-speaking production of *¿Quién le teme a Virginia
Woolf?* at Gramercy Arts Theatre.

1973
February: CBS Television airs the 1966 movie version, with a few minor deletions in dialogue. Attracts around thirty million viewers nationwide.

1974
June: BBC Radio broadcasts new, uncut radio production starring Elaine Stritch and Ray McAnally.
October: Washington DC revival at Arena Stage, dir. John Dillon. Cast includes Peg Murray as Martha and Dianne Wiest as Honey.

1976
April: Broadway revival opens at Music Box Theatre after try-outs in New Haven and Boston. Directed by the author, and again designed by William Ritman. Starring Colleen Dewhurst, Ben Gazzara. Critical raves but limited box-office interest: production closes in July.

1981
August: major British revival opens at London's National Theatre, directed by Nancy Meckler. Stars Paul Eddington and Margaret Tyzack, who replaced Joan Plowright as Martha after a try-out run in Bath. Plowright withdrew citing a throat infection.

1987
February: British revival at London's Young Vic Theatre, directed in the round by David Thacker. Stars Billie Whitelaw and Patrick Stewart. Closes after allocated four weeks: prospective West End transfer is abandoned owing to withdrawals of leads.

1989
October: Los Angeles revival at Doolittle Theatre, Hollywood, directed by the author. Stars Glenda Jackson, John Lithgow. Poorly received by critics and audiences.

1990

January: Albee's revival re-opens in Houston, Texas, with cast composed of understudies from Los Angeles production.

1996

5 September: major British revival opens at Almeida Theatre, London, directed by Howard Davies. Starring Diana Rigg, David Suchet, Lloyd Owen, Clare Holman. After four-week run, transfers to Aldwych Theatre in West End, where it runs for fixed period of four months.

1997

Major French revival in Paris, dir. Pierre Constant, with Marie-Christine Barrault and Jean-Pierre Cassel.

REFERENCES

Note: Where the undernoted press articles and reviews do not list page references, this is because the pieces were consulted in archived clippings files which have kept no record of the original newspaper page numbers. In other cases where information is incomplete, this is also because the clipped articles are missing title-pages, etc.

Albee, Edward 1960. *New York Times*, 15 February. Brief, unattributed clipping citing comments by playwright.
  1962. 'Which Theatre is the Absurd One?' *New York Times*, 25 February. Reprinted in *American Playwrights on Drama*, ed. Horst Frenz (New York: Hill & Wang, 1965), 168–74.
  1965. *Who's Afraid of Virginia Woolf?*, Harmondsworth: Penguin.
  1996. 'Thirty-Five Years On'. Programme note for Almeida Theatre's revival production.
Austin, J. L. 1962. *How to Do Things with Words*, Oxford: Clarendon.
Baker, Robb 1976. 'Surviving Without Paragraphs', *Soho Weekly News*, 15 April, 33, 36.
Barnes, Clive 1976. 'Stage: *Virginia Woolf* ', *New York Times*, 2 April, 20.
Barr, Richard 1970. Letter to Editor of *Variety*, published under heading 'Barr Denies Homo "Woolf" But Fonda & Burton's P. A. Details Another Version', 10 November.
Baxandall, Lee 1965. 'The Theater of Edward Albee', *Tulane Drama Review*, vol. 9, no. 4 (Summer), 19–40.
Bennett, Susan 1990. *Theatre Audiences: A Theory of Production and Reception*, London: Routledge.

Bigsby, C. W. E. (ed.) 1975. *Edward Albee: A Collection of Critical Essays*, Englewood Cliffs, New Jersey: Prentice Hall.

Bigsby, C. W. E. 1984. *Critical Introduction to Twentieth Century American Drama, Volume 2: Williams, Miller, Albee*, Cambridge University Press.

Bolton, Whitney 1968. 'Atelje 212 Troupe In *Virginia Woolf*', *New York Morning Telegraph*, 5 July.

Bone 1976. '*Who's Afraid of Virginia Woolf*? *Variety*, 3 March.

Boston Herald 1963. 'Who's Afraid? Not Censor', 4 September, C.1, 21.

Buckley, Tom 1976. 'Who's Afraid of Broadway? Not Ben Gazzara', *New York Times*, 23 May, 2.7.

Callenbach, Ernest 1966. 'Film Reviews: *Who's Afraid of Virginia Woolf? Film Quarterly* vol. 20, no. 1, 45–8.

Canby, Vincent 1966. '*Virginia Woolf* Given Code Seal', *New York Times*, 11 June.

Chapman, John 1962a. 'A Play Lies Under the Muck in *Who's Afraid of Virginia Woolf? New York Daily News*, 15 October, 46.

Chapman, John 1962b. 'For Dirty-Minded Females Only', *Sunday News*, 21 October, 2.1.

Christiansen, Richard 1970. 'Ivanhoe "Woolf" a knockout', *Chicago Daily News*, 23 September, 39.

Clum, John M. 1992. *Acting Gay: Male Homosexuality in Modern Drama*, New York: Columbia University Press.

Clurman, Harold 1962. 'Who's Afraid of Virginia Woolf?' Reprinted in Bigsby (ed.) 1975, 76–9.

Coe, Richard L. 1963. 'Nancy Kelly in Albee's Drama', unattributed review of road tour production at Washington DC's National Theatre.

Coleman, Robert 1962. 'The Play You'll Love or Loathe', *New York Mirror*, 15 October, 20.

Crosland, Susan 1996. 'Do we really hate our spouses like this?' *Daily Telegraph*, 12 November.

Crowther, Bosley 1966. 'Who's Afraid of Audacity?' *New York Times*, 10 July, 2.1, 10.

Dash, Thomas 1962. 'New Albee Work Searing, Scalding, Revealing Drama', *Women's Wear Daily*, 15 October.

Delingpole, James 1996. 'Who knows the real David Suchet?' *Daily Telegraph*, 24 September.

Demastes, William 1988. *Beyond Naturalism: A New Realism in the American Theatre*, Westport, Connecticut: Greenwood Press.

Derrida, Jacques 1982. *Margins of Philosophy*, trans. Alan Bass, Brighton: Harvester.

Dettmer, Roger 1970. 'Ivanhoe's "Woolf" the greatest', *Chicago Today*, 23 September.

Denzin, Norman K. 1991. *Images of Postmodern Society*, London: Sage.

Dewhurst, Colleen 1997. *Colleen Dewhurst: My Autobiography* (written with and completed by Tom Viola), New York: Scribner.

Drake, Sylvie 1989. 'Few Fears on This *Virginia Woolf* ', *Los Angeles Times*, 1 October, Calendar section, 4, 40, 49.

Driver, Tom F. 1964. 'What's the Matter with Edward Albee?' *The Reporter*, January. Reprinted in Kernan 1967: 99–103.

Dundy, Elaine 1964. 'Who's Afraid of Edward Albee?' *The Sunday Times*, 2 February, 26–8.

Elgee 1963. 'Hit Play Might "Scare" Audience', *Los Angeles Citizen News*, 13 November, C2.

Gardner, Paul 1962. 'Matinee Troupe Gives Albee Play', *New York Times*, 1 November.

Gardner, Paul 1963. 'Director Meshes 4 *Virginia Woolf* Casts', *New York Times*, 3 July.

Gassner, John 1963. ' *Who's Afraid of Virginia Woolf?* on L.P.' *S.R.*, 29 June, 39–40.

Gellert, Roger 1964. 'Sex-War Spectacular', *New Statesman*, 14 February, 262.

Gottfried, Martin 1967. *A Theater Divided: The Post-War American Stage*, Boston: Little Brown.

Gottfried, Martin 1976. '"Woolf" Returns With Same Bite', *New York Post*, 2 April.

Harris, Andrew B. 1994. *Broadway Theatre*, London: Routledge.

Harrison, Joan 1965. 'Retired Hurt . . . Virginia Woolf After 51 Weeks', *Daily Mail*, 3 December.

Herridge, Frances 1966. 'Albee Talks About *Virginia Woolf*', *New York Post*, 1 July, 24.

Hobe 1962. 'Shows on Broadway: *Who's Afraid of Virginia Woolf?* *Variety*, 17 October.

Hobson, Harold 1964. 'Mr. Albee's secret', *The Sunday Times*, 9 February, Review section, 33.

Hope-Wallace, Philip 1964. '*Who's Afraid of Virginia Woolf?* *Guardian*, 7 February, 11.

Hutcheon, Linda 1988. *A Poetics of Postmodernism*, London: Routledge.

Jacobi 1970. Review of Ivanhoe Theatre's *Who's Afraid of Virginia Woolf?*, Associated Press.

Jennings, C. Robert 1965. 'All for the love of Mike', *Saturday Evening Post*, 9 October, 86.

Jones, D. A. N. 1974. 'Bitches in the Woolf pack', *Radio Times*, 27 June, 10–11.

Kaplan, Donald M. 1965. 'Homosexuality and American Theatre: A Psychoanalytic Comment', *Tulane Drama Review* vol. 9, no. 3 (Spring), 24–55.

Kauffmann, Stanley 1966a. 'Homosexual Drama And Its Disguises', *New York Times*, 23 January, 2.1.

Kauffmann, Stanley 1966b. 'On the Acceptability of the Homosexual', *New York Times*, 6 February, 2.1.

Kauffmann, Stanley 1966c. 'Screen: Funless Games at George and Martha's', *New York Times*, 24 June.

Kelly, Kevin 1963. 'Blistering, Brilliant Drama by Edward Albee', *Boston Globe*, 3 September.

Kernan, Alvin B. (ed.) 1967. *The Modern American Theater: A Collection of Critical Essays*, Englewood Cliffs: Prentice Hall.

Kerr, Walter 1962a. 'First Night Report: *Who's Afraid of Virginia Woolf?* *New York Herald Tribune*, 15 October.

Kerr, Walter 1962b. 'Albee's Inferno: All is Malice', *New York Herald Tribune*, 21 October.

Kerr, Walter 1976. '*Virginia Woolf* – Sparks Still Fly', *New York Times*, 11 April, 2.1, 7.

Kilgallen, Dorothy 1962. 'Broadway Bulletin Board', *New York Journal-American*, 15 October.

Kissel, Howard 1976. 'The Theater: *Who's Afraid of Virginia Woolf? Women's Wear Daily*, 2 April, 51.

Kolin, Philip C. (ed.) 1988. *Conversations with Edward Albee*, Jackson and London: University Press of Mississippi.

Leff, Leonard J. 1980. 'A Test of American Film Censorship: *Who's Afraid of Virginia Woolf? Cinema Journal* vol. 19, no. 2, 41–55.

Leff, Leonard J. 1981. 'Play Into Film: Warner Brothers' *Who's Afraid of Virginia Woolf? Theatre Journal*, December, 453–66.

Lehman, Ernest 1976. Interviewed in *American Film* (fragment clipping; no title page). October, 43–6.

Leonard, Hugh 1964. '*Who's Afraid of Virginia Woolf? Plays and Players*, April, 32.

Lerner, Max 1962. 'Who's Afraid?' *New York Post*, 17 October.

Lewis, Peter 1964. 'They're all Afraid of Virginia Woolf', *Daily Mail*, 7 February.

Lightman, Herb 1966. 'The Dramatic Photography of *Who's Afraid of Virginia Woolf? American Cinematographer*, August, 530–3, 558–9.

Little, Stuart W., 'A Director's Double Trouble – Rehearsing 2 Casts for 1 Show', *New York Herald Tribune*, 11 October.

London Theatre Record 1981. Collected London press reviews of the National Theatre production of *Who's Afraid of Virginia Woolf?* (27 August–9 September), 438–41.

London Theatre Record 1987. Collected London press reviews of Young Vic production of *Who's Afraid of Virginia Woolf?* (12–25 February), 185–9.

London Theatre Record 1996. Collected London press reviews of the Almeida Theatre production of *Who's Afraid of Virginia Woolf?* (23 September–6 October), 1227–32.

McCarthy, Gerry 1987. *Edward Albee*, London: Macmillan.

McNally, Terrence 1982. 'Landmark Symposium: *Who's Afraid of Virginia Woolf?* Dramatists Guild Quarterly*, vol. 19, no.1 (Spring), 8–23.

Marker, Lise-Lone and Marker, Frederick J. 1982. *Ingmar Bergman: A Life in the Theatre*, Cambridge University Press.

Marowitz, Charles 1964. '*Who's Afraid of Virginia Woolf?* *Plays and Players*, April, 32, 34.

Mishkin, Leo 1966. '*Who's Afraid of Virginia Woolf?* a Stunner', *New York Morning Telegraph*, 24 June.

Mortimer, John 1966. 'Duet for marital torturers', *Observer*, 10 July, Review section.

Nadel, Norman 1962. 'Rose Theater Gives Two Virginia Woolfs', *New York World-Telegraph and Sun*, 1 November.

Nadel, Norman 1964. 'Cast Change Gives "Woolf" New Tone', *New York World-Telegraph and Sun*, 14 January, 10.

Nathan, David 1964. 'Savage and Superb', *London Daily Herald*, 7 February.

Newquist, Roy 1966. Film report (fragment; title-page missing), *McCall's*, June, 88–9.

Newsweek 1966, 'Who's Afraid. . .' 4 July, 84.

Novick, Julius 1976. 'It's Still the Best Play Since 1962', *Village Voice*, 12 April.

Oliver, Edith 1966. 'The Current Cinema: Yes, Yes', *New York*, 2 July.

Oppenheimer, George 1976. 'Albee Directs a Powerful "Woolf"', *Newsday*, 11 April.

Parker, Andrew and Sedgwick, Eve Kosofsky (eds.) 1995. *Performativity and Performance*, London: Routledge.

P.D.D. 1968 'Who's Afraid of Virginia Woolf?' *Women's Wear Daily*, 5 July.

P.H. 1964. '*Who's Afraid of Virginia Woolf?* *Theatre World*, March.

Pond, Elizabeth 1965. 'Albee Under Polish Lens', *Christian Science Monitor*, 24 April.

Powell, Dilys 1966. 'Home Front Battles', *Sunday Times*, 10 July.

Pryce-Jones, David 1964. 'The Rules of the Game', *Spectator*, 14 February, 213–14.

Rich, Alan 1976. 'The Survival of George and Martha', *New York*, 19 April.

Samuels, Steven 1994. 'Yes is Better Than No: an Interview with Edward Albee', *American Theatre*, September, 38.

Sarris, Andrew 1966. 'Films', *Village Voice*, 28 July.

Schechner, Richard 1963. 'Who's Afraid of Edward Albee?' *Tulane Drama Review* vol. 7, no. 3 (Spring), 7–10.

Schechner, Richard 1965. 'Reality Is Not Enough: An Interview with Alan Schneider', *Tulane Drama Review* vol. 9, no.3 (Spring), 143–50.

Schneider, Alan 1963. 'Why So Afraid?' *Tulane Drama Review* vol. 7, no. 3 (Spring), 10–13.

Schneider, Alan 1986. *Entrances: An American Director's Journey*, New York: Viking.

Simon, Francesca 1981. 'Who's Afraid of a Classic?' *The Sunday Times*, 5 July.

Smith, Cecil 1963. 'Nancy Kelly Afraid? Not of Virginia Woolf', *Los Angeles Times*, 10 November, Calendar section, 2.

Smith, Michael 1962. 'Theatre Uptown', *Village Voice*, 18 October, 11, 17.

Sontag, Susan 1964. 'Against Interpretation', reprinted in *A Susan Sontag Reader* (Harmondsworth: Penguin, 1983), 95–104.

Spector, Susan 1990. 'Telling the Story of Albee's *Who's Afraid of Virginia Woolf*?: Theatre History and Mythmaking', *Theatre Survey*, no. 31 (November), 177–99.

Stern, Daniel 1976. 'Albee: "I Want My Intent Clear"', *New York Times*, 28 March, 2.1, 5.

Sullivan, Dan 1968. 'Theater: Albee in Croatian', *New York Times*, 4 July, 13.

Sullivan, Dan 1989. 'A Lower-Key George and Martha', *Los Angeles Times*, 6 October, 4.1, 10.

Syse, Glenna 1970. '*Virginia Woolf* Is More Than It Used To Be', *Chicago Sun-Times*, 23 September, 71, 82.

Tallmer, Jerry 1963. 'Rediscovered Star', *New York Post*, 22 April.

Tallmer, Jerry 1965. '*Virginia Woolf* Is Revived at Paramus', *New York Post*, 16 June, 66.

Taubman, Howard 1962. 'The Theater: Albee's *Who's Afraid*', *New York Times*, 15 October.

Taubman, Howard 1963. 'Modern Primer: Helpful Hints to Tell Appearances vs. Truth', *New York Times*, 28 April, 2.1.

Thompson, Howard 1965. 'Unafraid of *Virginia Woolf*', *New York Times*, 5 September, 2.7, 10.

Thompson, Thomas 1966. 'Raw Dialogue Challenges All The Censors', *Life*, June [?] (undated clipping), 92, 96, 98.

The Times (London) 1964. 'Advanced Tactics in Marital Warfare', 7 February.

Trilling, Diana 1963. 'The Riddle of *Who's Afraid of Virginia Woolf?* Reprinted in Bigsby (ed.) 1975, 80–8.

Tyzack, Margaret 1981. 'Cut the Arty-Farty Cackle and Trust your Guts' (unattributed interview with the actress), *Guardian*, 22 August.

Variety 1963. 'Boston, the Cradle of Censorship, Trims *Virginia Woolf* as "Cesspool"; Dailies, Liberties Union Protest', 11 September, 84.

Wallace, Pat 1964. 'On Plays: The Marrow of Greatness', *Tatler*, 19 February, 382.

Watts, Richard 1968. 'The Yugoslav *Virginia Woolf*', *New York Post*, 5 July, 52.

Weatherby, W. J. 1962. 'Albee on Broadway', *Guardian*, 15 October, 7.

Whitelaw, Billie 1987. 'Billie's Afraid of Albee'. Unattributed interview in *The Sunday Times* (London), 6 February.

Whitelaw, Billie 1995. *Billie Whitelaw: Who He?*, London: Hodder and Stoughton.

Williams, Bob 1973. 'On the Air', *New York Post*, 23 February.

Wilson, Edwin 1976. 'Sound and Fury in a Living Room', *Wall Street Journal*, 7 April.

Zinman, Toby 1998. 'Beam me up, Patrick Stewart', *American Theatre*, vol. 15, no. 2 (February), 12–15, 68–70.

INDEX

absurd, theatre of the 82, 85, 185
acting methods 28, 29, 94, 132, 146–147,
    151, 157, 181
Actors Studio 19–20
Albee, Edward
    on absurdism/realism 82
    on actors 65, 67–68, 69, 149, 152, 161,
        171–172
    on censorship 43
    on critics 12, 83
    as director 62–68, 115, 118–119,
        134–135, 142–143, 150, 182
    on design 120–121, 129
    family background 106
    on film adaptation 58
    income 36, 46–47
    on homosexuality dispute 105–106,
        107
    on play in production 2, 4, 118–119,
        131, 143
    in rehearsal (1962) 31
    unpublished works 13, 106
    writing of *Who's Afraid . . .* 16–18,
        31–33, 128
Albery, Donald 44, 45
Aldwych Theatre (London) 74, 136
All the Way Home (Agee & Mosel) 26
All Over (Albee) 62
Almeida Theatre (London) 74, 115–116,
    120–121, 136, 163
American Dream, The (Albee) 16, 22,
    61
American Buffalo (Mamet) 113
American Psychiatric Association 102
Anderman, Maureen 130
Arena Stage (Washington DC) 61, 127
Artaud, Antonin 113
Atelje 212 66, 97–98, 107, 135
Austin, J.L. 5, 8
awards 41, 60

BBC radio adaptation (1974) 60, 136, 138,
    140, 163, 172, 184
Ballad of the Sad Cafe, The (McCullers/
    Albee) 29, 62
Baker, Robb 111, 150, 159
Barnes, Clive 65, 150
Barr, Richard 13, 20–21, 22, 23–25, 27, 35,
    36–38, 39, 43, 60, 62, 83, 107, 136,
    149
Baxandall, Lee 104, 124
Beatty, Warren 107
Beckett, Samuel 6, 11, 16, 22, 72, 73, 82,
    93, 94
Berghof, Herbert 26, 29
Bergman, Ingmar 39, 104, 121–122, 131
Bigsby, Christopher 32
Billington, Michael 98, 116, 152
Billy Rose Theatre (New York) 24
Bolton, Whitney 135
Braun, Pinkas 39–40
Broadway system 21–25, 34, 62, 83
Brown, Georgina 152
budgeting (1962 production) 24–25, 36
Burton, Richard 2, 3, 26, 50, 59, 90, 104,
    107, 140–141, 146, 153, 158–162,
    164–166, 171, 177, 181

CBS cast recording (1963) 37, 136–137,
    138, 145, 156, 169
Callenbach, Ernest 53, 59, 111
Cat on a Hot Tin Roof (Williams) 21, 75
censorship 42–46, 49, 54–58, 59
Chapman, John 19, 35, 79, 84, 99–100,
    102, 105
Clark, Kendall 37, 39
Clum, John 108–110, 172
Clurman, Harold 94–95, 122
Coleman, Robert 83–84, 98
Coward, Noel 35
Coveney, Michael 123

201